WHO SANG WHAT
ON THE SCREEN

ALAN WARNER

ANGUS
& ROBERTSON
PUBLISHERS

Photograph credits and acknowledgements
ABC Entertainment, Columbia Pictures, Hal Roach Studios, MGM/UA
Entertainment, Paramount Pictures, RKO General, The Samuel Goldwyn
Company, 20th Century-Fox, Universal Pictures, Walt Disney Pictures,
Warner Brothers and the following music publishers: Bourne And Co.,
Campbell Connelly, CBS Songs, Chappell & Co., Famous Music
Corporation, Screen Gems-EMI Music, Southern Music, and Warner Bros.
Music. Also MCA Records and EMI Records.

ANGUS & ROBERTSON PUBLISHERS

Unit 4, Eden Park, 31 Waterloo Road,
North Ryde, NSW, Australia 2113, and
16 Golden Square, London W1R 4BN,
United Kingdom

This book is copyright.
Apart from any fair dealing for the
purposes of private study, research,
criticism or review, as permitted
under the Copyright Act, no part may
be reproduced by any process without
written permission. Inquiries should
be addressed to the publishers.

First published in Australia
by Angus & Robertson Publishers in 1984
First published in the United Kingdom
by Angus & Robertson in 1984
Reprinted 1986

Copyright © Alan Warner 1984

National Library of Australia
Cataloguing-in-publication data.

Warner, Alan, 1943- .
  Who sang what on the screen.

  Includes index.
  ISBN 0 207 14869 4.

  1. Moving-picture music — United States — Dictionaries.
  2. Music, Popular (Songs, etc.) — United States — Dictionaries.
  I. Title.

782.8'5

Typeset in 10 pt Paladium by Setrite Typesetters
Printed in Singapore

FOREWORD

I heard about the legendary Alan Warner a week or two before I actually met him. This momentous coming together of two of the world's most devoted lovers of vinyl took place in EMI House, Manchester Square, London, in June 1966. I was a humble management trainee at EMI Records; Alan occupied a post the exact title of which I forget, but he definitely had clout in the department that listened to master tapes and discs that came from outside sources such as foreign (mainly American) labels and British independent record producers. In those days in the UK, the independent producer was just taking over from the in-house A and R man as the record business's most important source of product (remember that George Martin produced all the early Beatles hits as a salaried employee of EMI) and Alan's office was always a haven where EMI's juniors could hear interesting new sounds from both Britain and America. But even more gripping than the opportunity to hear sneak previews of new records bound for release on one of EMI's many UK labels was the chance to talk records with a record fanatic. Alan's knowledge of hits past (and, for that matter, flops) was, and is, staggering. I pride myself on my memory for names, titles, labels and events of the record world since the mid-fifties, but I fear I am probably not quite in Alan's league. Worse, he has this enormous expertise, enthusiasm and knowledge about *two* major fields of entertainment — he is as unstoppable when he reminisces about the cinema.

Since his stint at EMI, and before what I suppose was an inevitable move to Hollywood, Alan has held several important positions in UK record companies, and has been responsible for the reissue and repackaging of many important and fascinating recordings, for which every serious record collector has reason to be grateful. So many record companies either don't know what they've got (to paraphrase Ral Donner) in their vaults, or if they do they don't know what to do with it. Any company that has had Alan on its payroll for more than a few months has had the best possible use made of its catalogue, work Alan has done meticulously and out of love for the music. He has even produced massive hit singles in the UK with artists long since departed, such as his enormous number 2 UK hit in 1975 by Laurel and Hardy — "The Trail Of The Lonesome Pine". There must have been thousands of young record buyers who were introduced to the genius of Stan and Ollie that year by Alan's single.

Alan has put together memorable series of albums featuring all types and eras of popular music — and any album with his name on the cover as producer or coordinator means both the consumer and the original artist (not to mention the record company) get the very best service. Alan's series of albums *The Many Sides Of Rock 'n' Roll* remain some of the most-played sides in my (large) collection.

With this book, the Alan Warner legend takes another step forward. As he did with the Laurel and Hardy single, Alan has again brought together his two main passions — the cinema and popular music — to produce a stunning work. This time it's a book (as you will have already spotted). It is fun to read, and vital for research. It will soon be harder than ever to convince his followers he was not one of the original Warner Brothers.

Tim Rice
Great Milton,
Oxfordshire,
England

INTRODUCTION

In a 1940 movie titled *Arise My Love*, Claudette Colbert remarks to Ray Milland that "there's nothing like the sentiment you get from an old song". True enough, but so often, having heard a familiar melody, you find yourself trying to remember who originally sang the song, and where and when you first heard it.

This book is designed to nudge your memory and help you identify a few of those songs which we either grew up listening to, or are hearing for the first time, even though they probably date back a number of years.

I deal here mainly with American popular songs on record and film over the past fifty years and the majority of categories covered are done so selectively with no attempt at comprehensive listings. Unfortunately, songs in dramatic motion pictures often receive short shrift from reviewers and part of my reason for compiling this book was to put into accessible print facts about title and theme songs which have not all been readily available when I have tried to track them down myself.

While certain references to rock acts are included, I have not attempted to extensively list rock performers in the movie musicals section. Philip Jenkinson and I undertook a detailed study of that genre in *Celluloid Rock* (1974), and I strongly recommend two later publications, namely Fred Dellar's *NME Guide to Rock Cinema* (1982) and David Ehrenstein and Bill Reed's *Rock on Film* (1982).

My longstanding fascination with both music and movies as well as my ongoing fact filing system served me well in creating the basis for this study, though credit should also be given to the Margaret Herrick Library of the Academy of Motion Picture Arts and Sciences as well as to the myriad books which over the years have provided me with both reference and inspiration. Specific mention should be made of David Ewen's *American Popular Songs* (1966), Arthur Jackson and John Russell Taylor's *The Hollywood Musical* (1971), Nat Shapiro's six volumes of *Popular Music* (1973) and Roger D. Kinkle's *Complete Encyclopedia of Popular Music and Jazz, 1900–1950* (1974).

The sources for illustrative material included Eddie Brandt's "Saturday Matinee" in North Hollywood as well as my own collection. I thank Norman Moore for photographing the record sleeves and labels, and the film and record companies and music publishers whose posters, publicity stills and artwork provide such rewarding illustration throughout.

CONTENTS

1 WHO SANG WHAT... AND WHEN

Certain songs will forever be synonymous with those singers and musicians who made them famous.

"Paper Doll" (Black) will always be instantly linked with The Mills Brothers, "Broken-Hearted Melody" is the sole property of Sarah Vaughan, and the two words "Chances Are" (Allen–Stillman) spell only Johnny Mathis.

Here are some similarly immediate associations:

A-TISKET, A-TASKET (Fitzgerald–
  Feldman)
  Ella Fitzgerald (1938)
BE MY LOVE (Brodzsky–Cahn)
  Mario Lanza (1950)
CATCH A FALLING STAR (Vance–
  Pockriss)
  Perry Como (1958)
I LEFT MY HEART IN SAN FRAN-
  CISCO (Cory–Cross)
  Tony Bennett (1962)
LIPSTICK ON YOUR COLLAR
  (Goehring–Lewis)
  Connie Francis (1959)
LITTLE THINGS MEAN A LOT
  (Stutz–Lindeman)
  Kitty Kallen (1954)
MANANA (IS SOON ENOUGH FOR
  ME) (Barbour–Lee)
  Peggy Lee (1948)
MONA LISA (Livingston–Evans)
  Nat "King" Cole (1950)
MY PRAYER (Boulanger–Kennedy)
  The Platters (1956)
SO MANY WAYS (Stevenson)
  Brook Benton (1959)
STRANGERS IN THE NIGHT
  (Kaempfert–Snyder–Singleton)
  Frank Sinatra (1966)

TENDERLY (Gross–Lawrence)
  Rosemary Clooney (1952)

The record industry has always been competitive, and it is interesting to note that a few years ago, when a new song was published, it was not unusual for four or five major recordings of that single composition all to be vying for hit parade status.

To illustrate this, look at this sampling of three major songs and the recordings which gained hit status, all around the same time:

IT'S MAGIC (Styne–Cahn)
  (The song that Doris Day sang at
  the close of her first movie, 1948's
  Romance On The High Seas,
  which was released in the United
  Kingdom as *It's Magic*.)

Below: The Platters, supported by the Ernie Freeman Combo, sing "Only You" in *Rock Around The Clock* (1956). "The Great Pretender", from the same film, won for them a gold record.

"Mona Lisa", made famous by Nat "King" Cole, was featured in the film *Captain Carey, USA* (1950).

1948 hits: Doris Day
Dick Haymes
Gordon MacRae
Tony Martin
Sarah Vaughan

SOME ENCHANTED EVENING
(Rodgers–Hammerstein)
(One of the show-stoppers from *South Pacific*.)

1949 hits: Perry Como
Bing Crosby
Ezio Pinza
Jo Stafford
Frank Sinatra

UNCHAINED MELODY (North–Zareth)
(Based on the theme from the 1955 movie *Unchained*.)

1955 hits: Les Baxter And His Orchestra
Roy Hamilton
Al Hibbler
June Valli

(In the above listings, the artist who scored the biggest hit is shown first.)

One test of a great composition is its longevity, and a large number of popular tunes have second, third and maybe more lives as succeeding generations of performers keep the songs alive.

Here are some such songs which have bridged generation gaps and can now be counted as "standards". All artists shown below enjoyed hit parade status in the years indicated.

ALMOST LIKE BEING IN LOVE
(Loewe–Lerner) 1947
1954: Sung in the film *Brigadoon* by Gene Kelly
1978: Michael Johnson

BLUE MOON (Rodgers–Hart) 1934
1949: Mel Torme
1956: Elvis Presley
1961: The Marcels

CHATTANOOGA CHOO-CHOO
(Warren–Gordon) 1941
1941: Glenn Miller And His Orchestra (and featured in their film *Sun Valley Serenade*)
1978: Tuxedo Junction

DEEP PURPLE (Parish–DeRose) 1934
1957: Billy Ward And The Dominoes
1963: Nino Tempo And April Stevens
1976: Donny And Marie Osmond

GEORGIA ON MY MIND (Carmichael–Gorrell) 1930
c.1930: Mildred Bailey
1960: Ray Charles
1966: The Righteous Brothers
1978: Willie Nelson

GHOST RIDERS IN THE SKY
(originally RIDERS IN THE SKY)
(Jones) 1949
   1949: Vaughn Monroe
        Bing Crosby
        Burl Ives
   1961: The Ramrods
        Lawrence Welk
   1966: The Baja Marimba Band
   1980: Johnny Cash
   1981: The Outlaws

I DON'T WANT TO WALK WITH-
OUT YOU (Styne–Loesser) 1942
   1942: Sung in the film *Sweater
Girl* by Betty Jane Rhodes
and Johnnie Johnston
   1942: Harry James And His Orchestra with Helen Forrest
   1942: Bing Crosby
   1980: Barry Manilow

I ONLY HAVE EYES FOR YOU
(Warren–Dubin) 1934
   1934: Sung in the film *Dames* by
Dick Powell and Ruby
Keeler
   1959: The Flamingos
   1966: The Lettermen
   1975: Art Garfunkel

LOVE LETTERS (Young–Heyman) 1945
   1945: Theme from the film *Love
Letters*
   1962: Ketty Lester
   1966: Elvis Presley

MISTER SANDMAN (Ballard) 1954
   1954: The Chordettes
   1981: Emmylou Harris

OVER THE RAINBOW (Arlen–
Harburg) 1938
   1939: Sung in the film *The Wizard
Of Oz* by Judy Garland
   1960: The Dimensions
   1981: Jerry Lee Lewis

Judy Garland made
her first big hit with
this song from the
magical *The Wizard
Of Oz* (1939).

SINCE I DON'T HAVE YOU (Skyliners–Rock) 1959
   1959: The Skyliners
   1964: Chuck Jackson
   1970: Eddie Holman
   1979: Art Garfunkel
   1981: Don McLean

STARDUST (Carmichael–Parish) 1929
   1940: Artie Shaw
   1940: Tommy Dorsey
   1957: Billy Ward And The Dominoes
   1978: Willie Nelson (on his
"Stardust" album)

TRY A LITTLE TENDERNESS
(Woods – Campbell – Connelly)
1932
  c.1932: Ruth Etting
   1962: Aretha Franklin
   1966: Otis Redding
   1969: Three Dog Night

3

2 WHO SANG AND PLAYED THE BIG BAND HITS

Tracing the origins of many popular ballads played today, one inevitably comes across the swing era and those big bands which revolutionised dance music from the mid-1930s onwards.

The following is a selected list of melodies that have lingered on since they were first on the listings of "Your Hit Parade".

Understandably, not every song is able to transcend time barriers, but Barry Manilow's 1980 chart success with "I Don't Want To Walk Without You" is a perfect example of the durability of a first-class ballad.

Included with these familiar songs are a few of the instrumentals that became virtual anthems of the bands that featured them.

AND THE ANGELS SING (Elman–Mercer)
Benny Goodman with vocal by Martha Tilton (1939)
ARTISTRY IN RHYTHM (Kenton)
Stan Kenton (1943)

BEAT ME DADDY, EIGHT TO THE BAR (Raye–Sheehy–Prince)
Will Bradley, with Ray McKinley (1940)
BEGIN THE BEGUINE (Porter)
Artie Shaw, Tony Pastor (1938)
BIG NOISE FROM WINNETKA (Haggart – Barduc – Crosby – Rodin)
Bob Crosby (1940)

CHATTANOOGA CHOO-CHOO (Warren–Gordon)
Glenn Miller with Tex Beneke, Marion Hutton And The Modernaires (1941)
CHEROKEE (Noble)
Charlie Barnet (1939)

DON'T GET AROUND MUCH ANYMORE (Ellington–Russell)
Duke Ellington (1943)

FLYING HOME (Hampton–Goodman–Robin)
Lionel Hampton (1939)

GOODNIGHT SWEETHEART (Noble – Campbell – Connelly – Vallee)
Ray Noble, with Al Bowlly (1931)

I CAN'T GET STARTED (Duke–Gershwin)
Bunny Berigan (1937)
I DON'T WANT TO WALK WITHOUT YOU (Styne–Loesser)
Harry James, with Helen Forrest (1942)
I GOT IT BAD AND THAT AIN'T GOOD (Ellington–Webster)
Duke Ellington, with Ivie Anderson (1942)
I HAD THE CRAZIEST DREAM (Warren–Gordon)
Harry James, with Helen Forrest (1942)
I'LL NEVER SMILE AGAIN (Lowe)
Tommy Dorsey, with The Pied Pipers And Frank Sinatra (1940)
I'M BEGINNING TO SEE THE LIGHT (Ellington – James – Hodges – George)
Harry James, with Kitty Kallen (1945)

I'M GETTIN' SENTIMENTAL OVER YOU (Bassman–Washington)
Tommy Dorsey (1936)

I'VE GOT A GAL IN KALAMAZOO (Warren–Gordon)
Glenn Miller, with Tex Beneke, Marion Hutton And The Modernaires (1942)

I'VE HEARD THAT SONG BEFORE (Styne–Cahn)
Harry James, with Helen Forrest (1943)

IT ISN'T FAIR (Sprigato–Himber–Warshauer)
Sammy Kaye, with Don Cornell (1950)

JUKE BOX SATURDAY NIGHT (McGrane–Stillman)
Glenn Miller, with Tex Beneke, Marion Hutton And The Modernaires (1942)

LET'S DANCE (Stone–Bonime–Baldridge)
Benny Goodman (1939)

MARIE (Berlin)
Tommy Dorsey, with Jack Leonard (1937)

MINNIE THE MOOCHER (Calloway–Mills)
Cab Calloway (1932)

MOONLIGHT SERENADE (Miller–Parish)
Glenn Miller (1940)

NIGHTMARE (Shaw)
Artie Shaw (1938)

ON THE SUNNY SIDE OF THE STREET (McHugh–Fields)
Tommy Dorsey, with The Sentimentalists (1944)

ONE O'CLOCK JUMP (Basie)
Count Basie (1938)

PRAISE THE LORD AND PASS THE AMMUNITION (Loesser)
Kay Kyser (1942)

SATIN DOLL (Ellington)
Duke Ellington (1953)

SENTIMENTAL JOURNEY (Brown–Homer–Green)
Les Brown, with Doris Day (1945)

SERENADE IN BLUE (Warren–Gordon)
Glenn Miller, with Ray Eberle And The Modernaires (1942)

Glenn Miller featured "Serenade in Blue" and "I've Got a Gal in Kalamazoo", in *Orchestra Wives* (1942).

SING, SING, SING (Prima)
Benny Goodman (1937)

SO RARE (Herst–Sharpe)
Jimmy Dorsey (1938)
(Jimmy Dorsey successfully recut the tune in 1957.)

A STRING OF PEARLS (Gray–Delange)
Glenn Miller (1941)

A SUNDAY KIND OF LOVE (Rhodes–Prima–Belle–Leonard)

Claude Thornhill, with Fran Warren (1946)

TAKE THE "A" TRAIN (Strayhorn)
Duke Ellington (1941)

WHY DON'T YOU DO RIGHT? (McCoy)
Benny Goodman, with Peggy Lee (1942)

WOODCHOPPER'S BALL (Herman–Bishop)
Woody Herman (1939)

Always in the business of taking advantage of popular trends, Hollywood recruited many of the leading big bands (and a number of the lesser ones) to perform their hit parading songs in motion pictures. Some of these are listed in the "Movie Musical Songs"

section later in this book, but I should mention here that Benny Goodman and Peggy Lee performed "Why Don't You Do Right?" in 1943's *Stage Door Canteen*, while Bob Crosby And His Orchestra deliver their "Big Noise From Winnetka" hit in 1940's *Let's Make Music*, and Artie Shaw's "Nightmare" was heard in 1939's *Dancing Co-Ed*.

The major studios also produced series of one-reeler shorts showcasing the big bands of that same period, which were shown theatrically as part of the supporting programme. Probably the finest of these is 1939's *Symphony Of Swing* with Artie Shaw And His Orchestra; four numbers are featured including two vocals, namely "Deep Purple" (DeRose–Parish) sung by Helen Forrest, and "Jeepers

I'll Get By (1950), a remake of *Tin Pan Alley* (1941), featured one of Harry James's popular sellers of the 1940s, "It's Been A Long, Long Time". James (centre) was married to Betty Grable for 20 years.

Woody Herman and his Orchestra in *New Orleans* (1947), a film rarely seen, featuring the legendary Billie Holiday.

Creepers" (Warren–Mercer) delivered by Tony Pastor. "Begin The Beguine" was included in an earlier Artie Shaw filmlet.

Trumpeter Harry James (who can be spotted playing and singing with the Benny Goodman band in 1937's *Hollywood Hotel*) led his own orchestra in a number of pictures, mostly for MGM and 20th Century–Fox. James's wife, Betty Grable, was at that same time queen of the Fox lot and, in 1943, Hollywood's leading box-office star. Harry appeared in one of her musicals (1942's *Springtime In The Rockies*) as well as taking part in 1950's *I'll Get By*, which was a remake of an earlier Grable money-maker, 1940's *Tin Pan Alley*. Unfortunately, due to restrictions placed on Miss Grable by her studio, Mr and Mrs James only ever recorded one song commercially, "I Can't Begin To Tell You" (Monaco–

Gordon), and even then Betty's performance was credited to Ruth Haag.

In mid-1982 two records on the American singles chart offered contemporary medleys of big band hits, one by Frank Barber And His Orchestra, and the other and the more successful by Larry Elgart And His Manhattan Swing Orchestra. An alto-sax player with his brother's former band, Elgart had served brief stints with such as Woody Herman and Freddie Slack and, though his "Hooked On Swing" medley was performed with a minimum of excitement and verve, it nevertheless confirmed the ongoing popularity of such music and undoubtedly introduced its nostalgic style to a new age of listeners.

3 WHO SANG WITH WHOM

When the dance bands were in their prime, much rivalry existed between the various units and, somewhat like the exchange of manpower within professional football today, key players and vocalists moved around from group to group, creating a complicated web of personnel changes. To help remind you who sang with whom, here is a brief rundown of certain outstanding vocalists from the big band era along with the leading bands they fronted.

IVIE ANDERSON with Duke Ellington

DESI ARNAZ with Xavier Cugat
(Arnaz was later a bandleader himself.)

HARRY BABBITT with Kay Kyser
(Babbitt sang on such Kay Kyser hits as "Who Wouldn't Love You" and "Jingle, Jangle, Jingle", both in 1942. He was a regular member of Kyser's Kollege Of Musical Knowledge.)

MILDRED BAILEY with Paul Whiteman, Red Norvo

AL BOWLLY with Roy Fox, Ray Noble

JUNE CHRISTY with Stan Kenton
(Together they made "Tampico" one of the best-loved novelty songs of 1945.)

ROSEMARY CLOONEY with Tony Pastor
(Before her solo career began,

The Glenn Miller Orchestra as it appeared in *Sun Valley Serenade* (1941). Ray Eberle is in the centre of the five vocalists.

Rosemary and sister Betty — The Clooney Sisters — sang with saxman Tony Pastor's band.)

RUSS COLUMBO with Gus Arnheim
(Columbo worked briefly with Arnheim in 1929–30. He later became one of the greatest crooners with hits like "Prisoner Of Love" in 1931.)

PERRY COMO with Ted Weems
(He launched his solo career in 1944; his first hit was "Long Ago And Far Away".)

BING CROSBY (AND THE RHYTHM BOYS) with Paul Whiteman, Gus Arnheim
(The three Rhythm Boys, including young Crosby, sang with Whiteman in the 1930 *King Of Jazz* movie, and later with Arnheim at The Cocoanut Grove.)

DORIS DAY with Les Brown
(She sang "Sentimental Journey" and "Amapola" with the Band of Renown before launching into movies in 1948.)

RAY EBERLE with Glenn Miller
BOB EBERLY with Jimmy Dorsey
(He sang "Maria Elena" with Dorsey.)

FRANCES FAYE with Woody Herman
ELLA FITZGERALD with Chick Webb
("A-Tisket, A-Tasket" was the song that put Ella on the map in the late '30s.)
HELEN FORREST with Benny Goodman, Harry James, Artie Shaw

EYDIE GORME with Tex Beneke
MERV GRIFFIN with Freddy Martin
(Fronting Freddy Martin's Orchestra, the latterday television host sang Russ Morgan's "So

Ginny Simms sang with the Kay Kyser band. The Ziegfeld Follies introduced "I Can't Get Started" in 1936.

Tired", and "I've Got A Lovely Bunch Of Cocoanuts".)

CONNIE HAINES with Harry James, Tommy Dorsey
DICK HAYMES with Benny Goodman, Harry James, Tommy Dorsey
(Later solo best-sellers included "You'll Never Know" and "Little White Lies".)
HARRIET HILLIARD with Ozzie Nelson
(Hilliard sang "Get Thee Behind Me Satan" in the Astaire Rogers movie musical *Follow The Fleet* in 1935.)
BILLIE HOLIDAY with Count Basie, Artie Shaw
LENA HORNE with Noble Sissle, Charlie Barnet
HELEN HUMES with Count Basie
MARION HUTTON with Glenn Miller

KITTY KALLEN with Jimmy Dorsey, Harry James

Jo Stafford is credited as the first female solo singer to register record sales of over 25 million.

(Kallen later became a solo singer, topping the best-sellers in 1954 with "Little Things Mean A Lot".)

PEGGY LEE with Benny Goodman
(Her early solo career was highlighted by "Manana" which she wrote with husband Dave Barbour.)

HELEN O'CONNELL with Jimmy Dorsey
(She sang "Green Eyes" and "Amapola" with another Dorsey

vocalist, Bob Eberly.)
ANITA O'DAY with Stan Kenton
(Together they cut "And Her Tears Flowed Like Wine".)

JIMMY RUSHING with Count Basie

GINNY SIMMS with Kay Kyser
FRANK SINATRA with Harry James, Tommy Dorsey
(Stellar recordings with Dorsey And The Pied Pipers, including "There Are Such Things" and "I'll Never Smile Again".)

JO STAFFORD with Tommy Dorsey
(Member of The Pied Pipers, she also cut solo sides with Dorsey, including "Embraceable You" and "Yes, Indeed".)

KAY STARR with Charlie Barnet, Joe Venuti, Glenn Miller
(She began her solo career in the late '40s. Her biggest sellers were "Wheel Of Fortune" in 1952, and "Rock And Roll Waltz" in 1956.)

MARTHA TILTON with Benny Goodman

BEA WAIN with Larry Clinton

FRAN WARREN with Claude Thornhill

DINAH WASHINGTON with Lionel Hampton
(A formidable soul singer in her own right in the early '60s, singing "September In The Rain" and "What A Difference A Day Makes", plus some memorable duets with Brook Benton including "Baby, You Got What It Takes".)

JOE WILLIAMS with Count Basie

Janet Blair, a former band singer, was cast in *The Fabulous Dorseys* (1947) as the girl who grew up with the Dorseys in their struggle to the top.

"The Rock And Roll Waltz", recorded in 1956, was one of Kay Starr's biggest hits.

Note: Alice Faye, Betty Hutton, Marilyn Maxwell, Dale Evans, Dorothy Lamour, Gloria De Haven and Janet Blair were all band singers before they began their acting careers. Ironically, Janet Blair, who spent a short period with Hal Kemp's Orchestra prior to 1941, was cast as the girl who grew up with Tommy and Jimmy Dorsey in the 1947 biopic *The Fabulous Dorseys* and, appropriately, she sang. Her song was "To Me" (Wrubel–George).

4 THE VOCAL GROUPS

Vocal groups were also a significant spawning ground for major singing talents and it was from a male trio that one of the greatest popular singers of all time emerged, namely Bing Crosby who, with Al Rinker and Harry Barris, comprised The Rhythm Boys. Bing went on to cut, not just solo sides, but a number of duets linking him with The Andrews Sisters. He also worked from time to time with Connie Boswell, herself an alumnus of a three-sister singing group, The Boswell Sisters. However, if one had to be limited to singling out just four vocal teams of that period, the following would require specific mention.

THE ANDREWS SISTERS

Patty, Maxene and Laverne — one of the most popular all-time vocal groups, whose style has often been imitated. They appeared in various movies (often Abbott And Costello comedies) and certain of these credits appear later in this book. Their hit songs included "Rum And Coca-Cola" (Sullavan–Baron–Amsterdam), "Bei Mir Bist Du Schon (Means That You're Grand)" (Secunda–Jacobs–Chaplin–Cahn), and "I'll Be With You In Apple Blossom Time" (Von Tilzer–Fleeson).

One of the most popular vocal groups of all time, The Andrews Sisters. This scene is from *Hollywood Canteen*, made in 1944.

The Ink Spots influenced many later groups, particularly The Platters.

The Mills Brothers in *Cowboy Canteen* (1944).

13

The Pied Pipers first gained recognition when they recorded "There Are Such Things", performing with Tommy Dorsey And His Orchestra.

THE INK SPOTS

Bill Kenny, Charles Fuqua, Orville Jones and Ivory Watson — another vocal group that influenced many later outfits, particularly The Platters. Bill Kenny's lead tenor vocals introduced such hits as "If I Didn't Care" (Lawrence), "The Gypsy" (Reid), and "I Don't Want To Set The World On Fire" (Seiler–Marcus–Benjamin–Durham).

THE MILLS BROTHERS

Harry, Herbert, Donald and John were the original members until 1936, when brother John died and was replaced by John senior, the father of the group. Among the most memorable Mills Brothers hits are "Paper Doll" (Black), "Glow Worm" (Robinson–Lincke–Mercer), and "You Always Hurt The One You Love" (Roberts–Fisher).

THE PIED PIPERS

Originally a male team, it became an eight-piece when female singer Jo Stafford joined them. Their most famous line-up in the early '40s was a foursome, comprising Miss Stafford, John Huddleston, Chuck Lowry and Clark Yocum. June Hutton (sister of Marion Hutton) took over the female vocals when Jo Stafford began her solo career, and the Pipers recorded with Johnny Mercer. The songs most closely associated with the group are "There Are Such Things" (Meyer – Adams – Baer) which they recorded with Tommy Dorsey And His Orchestra (with whom they first achieved attention) and Frank Sinatra, "Dream" (Mercer), and "The Trolley Song" (Martin–Blane).

5 SONGS BASED ON THE CLASSICS

While many of the songs that the groups sang in the swing era are still being performed today, there is another source of composition that dates back even further. Songwriters have never been able, it seems, to resist "borrowing" from the great classical masters. What follows is a selection of songs derived from famous pieces, along with a couple of instrumental adaptations, restyled in conjunction with their use in motion pictures, a more recent example of which is Richard Strauss's "Also Sprach Zarathustra", played in its original orchestral form in 1968's *2001: A Space Odyssey*, and later adapted by Emuir Deodato for a pop single, which itself was utilised on the soundtrack of 1979's *Being There*.

ALL BY MYSELF (Carmen)
    Based on Rachmaninoff's Piano Concerto No. 2.
    Recorded by Eric Carmen (1976).
ALONE AT LAST (Lehmann)
    Based on Tchaikovsky's Piano Concerto No. 1.
    Recorded by Jackie Wilson (1960).
AN AMERICAN TUNE (Simon)
    Based on a melody from Bach's St. Matthew Passion.
    Recorded by Paul Simon (1973).

CAN'T HELP FALLING IN LOVE (Weiss–Peretti–Creatore)
    Based on the French melody "Plaisir D'Amour" (Martini).
    First recorded and sung by Elvis Presley in his 1962 film *Blue Hawaii*.

COULD IT BE MAGIC (Manilow–Anderson)
    Based on Chopin's Prelude in C Minor.
    Recorded by Barry Manilow (1975).

DON'T YOU KNOW (Worth)
    Based on Musetta's Waltz from Puccini's opera *La Bohème*.
    Recorded by Della Reese (1959).

FULL MOON AND EMPTY ARMS (Kaye–Mossman)
    Based on Rachmaninoff's Piano Concerto No. 2.
    Recorded by Frank Sinatra (1946).

HELLO MUDDAH, HELLO FADDAH (Sherman)
    Based on Ponchielli's "Dance Of The Hours".
    Recorded by Allan Sherman (1963).
HUMORESQUE
    Based on the Dvorak melody.
    Recorded by Guy Lombardo And His Royal Canadians (1946); concurrent with it being used as the theme for the Joan Crawford movie *Humoresque*.

I THINK OF YOU (Marcotte–Elliott)
    Based on Rachmaninoff's Piano Concerto No. 2.
    Recorded by Tommy Dorsey And His Orchestra, with Frank Sinatra (1941).
I'M ALWAYS CHASING RAINBOWS (Carroll–McCarthy)
    Based on Chopin's "Fantaisie

Impromptu".
Recorded by Perry Como (1946), and by Dick Haymes and Helen Forrest (1946).

IF YOU ARE BUT A DREAM (Jaffe–Fulton–Bonx)
Based on Rubinstein's "Romance".
Recorded by Jimmy Dorsey And His Orchestra (1941).

THE LAMP IS LOW (Parish–DeRose–Shefter)
Based on a theme from Ravel's "Pavanne".
Recorded by Larry Clinton And His Orchestra (1939).

A LOVER'S CONCERTO (Randell–Linzer)
Based on Bach's Minuet in G.
Recorded by The Toys (1965).

MINUTE WALTZ (O'Kun)
Based on Chopin's Minute Waltz.
Recorded by Barbra Streisand (1966).

MOON LOVE (Kostelanetz–David)
Based on the second movement of Tchaikovsky's Symphony No. 5.
Recorded by Glenn Miller And His Orchestra, with Ray Eberle (1939).

MY REVERIE (Clinton)
Based on Debussy's "Reverie".
Recorded by Larry Clinton And His Orchestra, with Bea Wain (1938).

NO OTHER LOVE (Weston–Russell)
Based on Chopin's Etude in E Major.
Recorded by Jo Stafford (1950).

NOW AND FOREVER (Savitt–Stillman)
Based on Tchaikovsky's Pathétique Symphony (No. 6).
Recorded by Freddy Martin And His Orchestra (1942).

OUR LOVE (Clinton)
Based on Tchaikovsky's Romeo and Juliet Overture.
Recorded by Larry Clinton And His Orchestra (1939).

PAINTER
Based on "One Fine Day" from Puccini's Madame Butterfly.
Recorded by Lou Christie (1966).

A SONG OF JOY (ODE TO JOY) (Orbe–De Los Rios–Parker)
Based on Beethoven's Symphony No. 9.
Recorded by Miguel Rios (1970).

A SONG OF LOVE (Romberg–Donnelly)
Based on a theme from Schubert's Unfinished Symphony.
Recorded by Jeanette MacDonald and Nelson Eddy (1936).

THE STORY OF A STARRY NIGHT (Livingston–Hoffman–Curtis)

"And This Is My Beloved", "Stranger in Paradise" and other *Kismet* songs were based on themes by the Russian composer, Borodin.

AND THIS IS MY BELOVED
Words and Music by ROBERT WRIGHT and GEORGE FORREST
Based on themes of A. Borodin

Charles Lederer
presents
ALFRED DRAKE
in Edwin Lester's production of
the Broadway Musical

KISMET

BOOK BY
CHARLES LEDERER and LUTHER DAVIS
(Based on a play by Edward Knoblock)

DIRECTED BY
ALBERT MARRE

DANCES AND MUSICAL NUMBERS STAGED BY
JACK COLE

SETTINGS AND COSTUMES DESIGNED BY
LEMUEL AYERS

From the Score
AND THIS IS MY BELOVED
HE'S IN LOVE
STRANGER IN PARADISE
BAUBLES, BANGLES AND BEADS
NIGHT OF MY NIGHTS
SANDS OF TIME

FRANK MUSIC AFFILIATES

Based on the first movement of Tchaikovsky's Pathétique Symphony.

Recorded by Glenn Miller And His Orchestra with Ray Eberle (1942).

STRANGER IN PARADISE (Wright–Forrest)

From the Broadway musical *Kismet*, the score of which was based on themes from Borodin's Polovtsian Dances. Sung in the show by Richard Kiley and Doretta Morrow (1953); in the film by Vic Damone and Ann Blyth (1955). Recorded by Tony Bennett (1953), The Four Aces (1953) and Tony Martin (1953).

THE THINGS I LOVE (Harris–Barlow)

Based on Tchaikovsky's Pathétique Symphony.

Recorded by Jimmy Dorsey And His Orchestra (1941).

THIS DAY OF DAYS

Based on Chopin's Etude No. 3.
Recorded by Jerry Vale.

TILL THE END OF TIME (Kaye–Mossman)

Based on Chopin's Polonaise.

Recorded by Perry Como (1945), and the theme subsequently used on the soundtrack and as the title of a 1946 movie *Till The End Of Time*.

TO LOVE AGAIN (Stoloff–Sidney–Washington)

Chopin's E Flat Nocturne adapted as the theme tune for the 1956 biopic of the 1930s pianist, *The Eddy Duchin Story*. Carmen Cavallaro dubbed the piano playing for Tyrone Power in the title role.

TONIGHT IS SO RIGHT FOR LOVE (Wayne–Silver)

Based on barcarolle from Offenbach's *Tales of Hoffman*.

Recorded by Elvis Presley on the soundtrack of his film *GI Blues* (1960).

TONIGHT WE LOVE (Martin–Austin–Worth)

Based on Tchaikovsky's Piano Concerto No. 1.

Recorded by Freddy Martin And His Orchestra, with Clyde Rogers (1941); by Tony Martin (1941). Also recorded by Freddy Martin And His Orchestra as "Piano Concerto In B Flat" (1941).

"Tonight We Love" is, in fact, only one of a number of lyrics given to Tchaikovsky's Piano Concerto No. 1 over the years. Another theme with alternative vocal versions is Richard Addinsell's "Warsaw Concerto", the piano piece "played" by Anton Walbrook in 1941's *Dangerous Moonlight* (US: *Suicide Squadron*). In the late 1950s, Carl Sigman wrote the lyric, "The

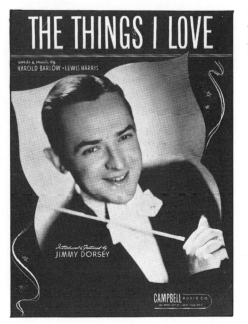

"The Things I Love" was recorded by Jimmy Dorsey in 1941.

The birth of the "Warsaw Concerto". Anton Walbrook at the keyboard in *Dangerous Moonlight* (1941).

"Tonight Is So Right For Love" was based on an Offenbach theme in *GI Blues* (1960), starring Elvis Presley and Juliet Prowse.

World Outside", which became a best-selling song for both The Four Coins and The Four Aces. However, Leslie Bricusse provided a second lyric more than two decades later and the song "The Precious Moments" (recorded by Matt Monro) was heard in yet another motion picture, 1980's *The Sea Wolves*.

6 THE HOLLYWOOD CHOIRS

Do you remember, in 1938's *Angels With Dirty Faces*, after racketeer James Cagney has been taken to the electric chair, Father Pat O'Brien and the Dead End Kids walking off together to the accompaniment of an angelic choir on the soundtrack? That was actually one of a few choral groups that Hollywood used extensively, the cherubic voices belonging to The Robert Mitchell Boychoir, credited in *Angels* as "The St Brendan's Church Choir", and in the same year's *Carefree* as "The St Brendan's Boys".

Tony Butala of The Lettermen started his career as a member of this choir, as did Alan Copeland of The Modernaires, plus all three of The Sandpipers. Among the many other films in which the Mitchell outfit was heard are 1942's *Joan Of Paris*, 1943's *Sweet Rosie O'Grady*, 1944's *Going My Way*, 1946's *The Jolson Story*, and 1947's *The Bishop's Wife*.

There were also St Luke's Choristers (led by William Ripley Door) made up of both young and older male voices, who sang with Shirley Temple in *Bright Eyes* (1934), with Bing Crosby in *The Bells Of St Mary's* (1945), and in the wartime drama, *Mrs Miniver* (1942).

Switch now to the classic Frank Capra comedy *Meet John Doe* (1941), and the triumph of the John Doe movement, personified by Gary Cooper's Long John Willoughby; aiding and abetting the Dimitri Tiomkin score is

Robert Mitchell directs Penny Singleton and the St Brendan's Choir in *Blondie In Society* (1941).

Welsh singers, select-
ed and directed by
Tudor Williams, as
they appeared in
*How Green Was My
Valley* (1941).

the choral arrangement of the theme
from Beethoven's 9th Symphony, sung
by The Hall Johnson Choir, led by
arranger–conductor Hall Johnson. The
same choir of forty voices was seen and
heard singing with Paul Robeson in
1942's *Tales Of Manhattan* and in
1943's *Cabin In The Sky*, as well as
being audible throughout another all-
black vehicle, *The Green Pastures*, in
1936, in which they voiced a whole
series of spirituals.

These choirs ran up extensive
movie credits, but one memorable
choral unit was assembled for just one
film appearance. In 1941 director John
Ford began shooting the movie version
of Richard Llewellyn's novel set in a
Welsh mining community, *How Green
Was My Valley*. 20th Century–Fox
built a complete village in California's
San Fernando Valley and began
searching for suitable Welsh singers,
finally deciding to use members of a
choir from the Welsh Presbyterian
Church in Los Angeles. For many of us

the memory of that compelling film
adaptation is synonymous with the
rich tone of male voices singing "Men
Of Harlech".

Before leaving choral performances on movie soundtracks, we
must remember the many United States
cavalry songs, such as "Garry Owen",
featured to great effect in 1941's *They
Died With Their Boots On*, and later in
1968's *Custer Of The West*. *She Wore A
Yellow Ribbon* in 1949 is perhaps the
best-known title song use of a cavalry
tune, though an earlier John Ford
western, 1946's *My Darling Clemen-
tine*, used an equally legendary folk-
song. Stan Jones composed "I Left My
Love" which the soundtrack chorus
sings under the titles of 1959's *The
Horse Soldiers*, and The Sons Of The
Pioneers contributed to several Ford
pictures, most notably 1950's *Wagon
Master*.

7 THERE GOES THAT SONG AGAIN

Popular songs have played a fascinating role in motion pictures — not just in the large-scale movie musical sequences, but via countless ways in which recognisable melodies have woven in and out of soundtracks.

During the golden years of the 1930s and 1940s, when Hollywood was in its heyday, movies were particularly interesting from a musical point of view because the major studios owned the copyright of many of the songs written for their musical productions. Consequently, when identifiable melodies were required for dramatic pictures, the producers would initially turn to the studio's song catalogue.

For instance, when marine Guy Madison returns home from the war in RKO's 1946 film *Till The End Of Time*, the radio is playing "Where Does Love Begin", a Jule Styne–Sammy Cahn song that Gloria De Haven introduced two years earlier in RKO's *Step Lively* musical.

Similarly, in the FBI drama *G-Men* in 1935, James Cagney goes into a nightclub and two of the musical numbers heard in the background ("I'm Going Shopping With You" and "Lullaby Of Broadway") come from that same year's (and same studio's) score by Harry Warren and Al Dubin, for the latest in the *Gold Diggers* cycle. Knowledge of this practice makes for interesting observation when viewing reruns on the late, late show!

Radios are one of the frequently used methods of introducing a background song into dramatic scenes; the many examples range from the romantic

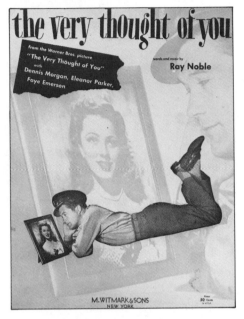

A 1944 reprint of this sheet music tied in a Warner Brothers movie of the same name. The song was later sung by Doris Day in *A Young Man With A Horn* (1950).

vocal of "The Very Thought Of You" (Noble) emanating from the car radio as Dennis Morgan falls in love with Eleanor Parker in the 1944 film bearing that song's title, to the pulsating rockbeat of "Machine Gun" (Storm) by Storm, blasting away on Kristy McNichol's transistor radio in *Only When I Laugh* (1981). In 1957's *The Great Man* Julie London sings along with her own recording of "The Meaning Of The Blues" (Troup–Worth) as it comes over the radio; and, in a memorable postcredit sequence in 1934's *Twenty Million Sweethearts* that sets the scene for this comedy–musical about broadcasting, a series of eight ornate receivers are shown in closeup as The Three Radio Rogues imitate such

21

The original advertisement for *Penny Serenade* of 1941. RCA ran a campaign ahead of the picture's release, advertising that the songs were available on Victor and Bluebird records.

come to mind include the one in which the juke plays "I'll See You In My Dreams" (Jones–Kahn) as Irene Dunne majestically descends a staircase toward a waiting Spencer Tracy in *A Guy Named Joe* (1943) and, five years earlier in *Mannequin*, the same Mr Tracy asks Ralph Morgan to put a nickel into the machine which subsequently plays "Always And Always" (Ward–Forrest–Wright) and to which Joan Crawford vocalises.

This leads us quite naturally to the phonograph, where again there are myriad examples to choose from. 1941's *Penny Serenade* is a prime contender for the best cinematic use of phonograph records in which the storyline is linked by more than a dozen standard songs, including "My Blue Heaven" (Donaldson–Whiting), "Just A Memory" (DeSylva–Brown–Henderson), "Moonlight And Roses" (Moret–Black) and "Together" (De-Sylva–Brown–Henderson); some of these melodies visually accompany scene changes by means of actual shots of early Victor discs, though the tracks used were recorded specially for the picture.

In an early sequence, Cary Grant enters a record store where Irene Dunne is an assistant; a vocal version of "You Were Meant For Me" is playing in the shop, complete with a repetitive fault, causing the disc to continually repeat one particular phrase! Grant buys a number of records purely to substantiate his remaining near to Miss Dunne, after which he confesses that he does not even own a Victrola!

Apparently, the studio searched for and found a fox terrier resembling the famous Nipper dog in the trademark of RCA Victor (The Gramophone Company in England) just for one closeup shot in the film.

popular entertainers of the day as Bing Crosby, Morton Downey, Kate Smith, Rudy Vallee and Arthur Tracy.

Jukeboxes have also been evident in many a film and two instances that

In an unrelated but equally significant use of a phonograph record, Joan Fontaine and Joseph Cotten, stranded on the Isle of Capri in their 1950 romantic adventure *September Affair*, are given a case of old 78 discs. They choose one, place it on the machine, and the voice of Walter Huston is heard singing "September Song" (Weill–Anderson). Huston — the actor and father of John — originally sang this song in the 1938 stage version of the *Knickerbocker Holiday* musical; another famous Hollywood character actor, Charles Coburn, sang it in the 1944 film version of *Knickerbocker Holiday*, and Maurice Chevalier revived it in the 1961 movie *Pepe*.

The generation gap becomes evident in 1958's *Andy Hardy Comes Home* when youngsters find some records owned by "Uncle" Mickey Rooney, including one of Shep Fields And His Rippling Rhythm, which they play and then instantly discard. Similarly, back in 1946, when Frank Sinatra was a bobbysox idol, a teenage daughter in the movie *Margie* discovers Rudy Vallee's record "My Time Is Your Time" (Dance–Hopper) and speculates whether Mr Vallee was a comparable idol in her mother's day!

You may also recall a gramophone playing "Buffalo Gals Can You Come Out Tonight" (Traditional) as James Stewart calls on Donna Reed in 1947's *It's A Wonderful Life*, and even Kirk Douglas opening up and playing a birthday gift of Brahms's Concerto in B Flat, the record itself accompanied by the inscription, "If music be the food of love — play on" and signed "Addie", the mysterious unseen character in 1949's *A Letter To Three Wives*. And it is to Fred Astaire's recording of "That

Face" (Spence–Bergman), that William Holden sweeps Audrey Hepburn off her feet in 1964's *Paris When It Sizzles*, a tongue-in-cheek nod to the earlier Astaire–Hepburn partnership in *Funny Face*.

Here are four occasions when performers on-screen "sing along" with visible phonograph records:

In 1949's *My Dream Is Yours*, Doris Day sings the first-ever lyric to the instrumental favourite "Canadian Capers" (Chandler–White–Cohen–Blane).

In 1975's *Lucky Lady*, Burt Reynolds vocalises with Fats Waller's classic, "Ain't Misbehavin'".

In 1954's *Sabrina*, Audrey Hepburn briefly joins in the lyric of "Yes, We Have No Bananas" (Cohn–Silver).

In 1979's *All That Jazz*, Ann Reinking and Erzsebet Foldi sing and dance to Peter Allen's own live recording of "Everything Old Is New Again" (Allen–Sager).

Before we leave the roles taken by record-playing machinery, mention must be made of the disc-jockey's turntable in Clint Eastwood's *Play Misty*

More than a dozen songs, including "My Blue Heaven", were recorded for *Penny Serenade* (1941), starring Irene Dunne and Cary Grant. The uncredited soundtrack vocalist was Johnnie Johnston.

Audrey Hepburn and William Holden in *Paris When It Sizzles* (1964).

Andrey Hepburn is swept off her feet by William Holden to Fred Astaire's recording of "That Face" in *Paris When It Sizzles* (1964).

For Me (1971). Erroll Garner's own recording of his legendary composition, "Misty", was prominently featured, as was Roberta Flack's million-selling "The First Time Ever I Saw Your Face" (MacColl).

8 IT'S THE SAME OLD SONG

In subsequent chapters, you will find reference to a great many established songs which have been re-recorded for use in motion pictures. It is of course an old practice for movie composers to integrate well-known melodies within the framework of contemporary scores. However, this section deals briefly with the element of source music, the use of which has become accentuated over the past few years.

To create an accurate musical framework, producers often select and license original commercial recordings, relevant to the specific timeframe of the screenplay.

The following is a representative list of recent films which have successfully adopted this policy and which, in each case, have utilised a whole collection of "golden oldies".

ALICE DOESN'T LIVE HERE ANY-MORE (1975)
Includes rock tracks such as "All The Way From Memphis" (Hunter) by Mott The Hoople, "Daniel" (John–Taupin) by Elton John, and "Jeepster" (Bolan) by T-Rex, plus two soundtrack oldies, "You'll Never Know" (Warren–Gordon) by Alice Faye from 1943's *Hello, Frisco, Hello* and "Cuddle Up A Little Closer" by Betty Grable from 1943's *Coney Island*.

AMERICAN GRAFFITI (1973)
Almost forty classic rock singles of the 1950s and early 1960s, including "Why Do Fools Fall In Love" (Lymon–Levy) by Frankie Lymon And The Teenagers, "Crying In The Chapel" (Glenn)

by Sonny Till And The Orioles, "Runaway" (Shannon–Crook) by Del Shannon and "All Summer Long" (Wilson) by The Beach Boys; one of the most effective cinematic uses of vintage rock music, aided by on-screen appearances of the Kim Fowley-produced Flash Cadillac And The Continental Kids.

COMING HOME (1978)
Set in 1968, this drama utilised just under twenty significant hits of the period, including "Hey Jude" (Lennon–McCartney) and "Strawberry Fields Forever" (Lennon–McCartney) by The Beatles, "Jumpin' Jack Flash" (Jagger–Richard) by The Rolling Stones, "Call On Me" (Malone) by Big Brother And The Holding Company featuring Janis Joplin, and "Born To Be Wild" (Bonfire) by Steppenwolf.

DINER (1982)
Includes "Dream Lover" (Darin) by Bobby Darin, "It's All In The Game" (Dawes–Sigman) by Tommy Edwards, "A Teenager In Love" (Pomus–Shuman) by Dion And The Belmonts, and "Don't Be Cruel" (Blackwell–Presley) by Elvis Presley.

THE LAST PICTURE SHOW (1971)
Songs from the 1950s including "Blue Velvet" (Morris–Wayne) by Tony Bennett, "Rose, Rose I Love You" (Thomas) by Frankie Laine, and "Please Mr Sun" (Getzov–Frank) by Johnnie Ray, plus a

Two of the many favourites from the 1950s featured on the soundtrack of *The Last Picture Show* (1971).

selection of Hank Williams songs as originally recorded by Williams himself.

LOOKING FOR MR GOODBAR (1977)

Contemporary rock/soul hits such as "Love Hangover" (Sawyer–McLeod) by Diana Ross, "Back Stabbers" (Huff–McFadden–Whitehead) by The O'Jays, "Low-down" (Skaggs–Paich) by Boz Scaggs, and "Don't Leave Me This Way" (Gamble–Huff–Gilbert) by Thelma Houston.

MEAN STREETS (1973)

Intriguing melange of operatic recordings and such rock/soul hits as "Please Mr Postman" (Holland–Gorman–Bateman) by The Marvelettes, "Be My Baby" (Spector–Greenwich–Barry) by The Ronettes, "Pledging My Love" (Robey–Washington) by Johnny

Ace and "Tell Me" (Jagger–Richards) by The Rolling Stones.

PAPER MOON (1973)

A host of 1930s favourites including "Just One More Chance" (Johnston–Coslow) by Bing Crosby, "Georgia On My Mind" (Carmichael–Gorrell) by Hoagy Carmichael, plus, of course, "It's Only A Paper Moon" (Arlen–Rose–Harburg) by Paul Whiteman and his Orchestra.

PORKY'S (1981)

Another 1950s collection including "Only You" (Ram) by The Platters, "How High The Moon" (Louis–Hamilton) by Les Paul and Mary Ford, "Tennessee Waltz" (King) by Patti Page, "Sh-Boom" (Keys) by The Crew-Cuts, and three Hank Williams classics, among them "Your Cheatin' Heart" and "Cold, Cold Heart".

RAGING BULL (1981)

A rich selection of classical music (the film's main theme is based on Mascagni's "Cavalleria Rusticana") and popular songs comprising "That's My Desire" (Kresa–Loveday) by Frankie Laine, "Prisoner of Love" (Columbo–Gaskill–Robin) by both Russ Columbo and Perry Como, "Frenesi" (Dominguez) by Artie Shaw, "Cow-Cow Boogie" (De-Paul–Carter–Raye) by Ella Fitzgerald and The Ink Spots, plus Marilyn Monroe singing "Bye Bye Baby" (Styne–Robin) as she did in *Gentlemen Prefer Blondes* in 1953.

RED SKY AT MORNING (1970)

Wartime songs including "Don't Sit Under The Apple Tree" (Brown–Tobias–Stept) by The Andrews Sisters, "Paper Doll" (Black) by The Mills Brothers, and "Oh Johnny, Oh Johnny Oh!" (Olman–Rose) by Benny Carter's Orchestra with Miriam Gulager.

THAT'LL BE THE DAY (1973)

This, with its successor *Stardust* (1974), was the British equivalent of the *American Graffiti* cycle. *That'll Be The Day* covered much of the same time period as the first *Graffiti* did, and likewise bore a soundtrack filled to the brim with golden oldies by such as Little Richard ("Tutti Frutti": Penni-man–Bostrie–Lubin) and The Everly Brothers ("Bye Bye Love": Bryant). Unfortunately, clearance to use Buddy Holly could not be obtained and so the soundtrack filled the gap by using Bobby Vee's version of the title song (Petty–Holly–Allison).

THE WANDERERS (1979)

Another soundtrack packed tight with rock hits, including "Soldier Boy" (Dixon–Green) by The Shirelles, "Stand By Me" (Lieber–Stoller–King) by Ben E. King, and three cuts by The Four Seasons including "Sherry" (Gaudio) and "Big Girls Don't Cry" (Crewe–Gaudio).

There are, by contrast, many films which only use a handful of popular recordings, and in some cases these are woven into the overall soundtrack so as to appear unobtrusive and some-times are difficult to detect; a case in point is Slim Whitman's "Love Song Of The Waterfall" (Nolan–Barnes–Winge) which is integrated into 1977's *Close Encounters Of The Third Kind*, the same song that was, incidentally, first introduced in a movie by Eddie Dean in 1947's *Romance Of The West*.

Just the mere mention of the 1955

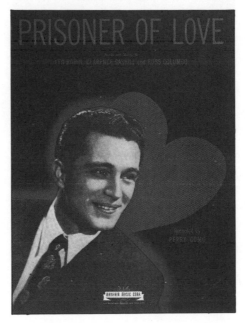

"Prisoner of Love" was featured on the soundtrack of *Raging Bull* (1981).

Bill Haley and his Comets in a publicity pose for "Rock Around The Clock" (1956). The use of that song on the sound-track of *Blackboard Jungle* in 1955 marked the official entry of rock 'n' roll into movies.

film *Blackboard Jungle* will bring to mind for many of us the effective use of "Rock Around The Clock" (De-Knight–Freeman) by Bill Haley And His Comets over the opening titles; what is not so readily remembered is that the soundtrack also featured two other commercial recordings, namely, "The Jazz-Me-Blues" by Bix Beider-becke And His Gang, and Stan Kenton's "Invention For Guitar And Orchestra And Trumpet".

In addition to the Alice Faye and Betty Grable tracks listed above as being used in *Alice Doesn't Live Here Anymore*, other performances from vintage Hollywood musicals have been lifted for use in later dramatic pictures, including Gene Kelly's classic title sequence from 1952's "Singin' In The Rain" (Brown–Freed) which is heard as the playout music in 1971's *A Clockwork Orange*, and similarly, Shirley Temple's original rendition of "On The Good Ship Lollipop" (Whiting–Clare) as first heard in 1934's *Bright Eyes*, re-emerged in 1976's *The Bingo Long Traveling All-Stars And Motor-Kings*.

One of the most regularly featured vocalists on movie soundtracks is Frank Sinatra, whose recording of "Have Yourself A Merry Little Christmas" (Martin–Blane) provided a poignant moment, accompanying the scene in which an American soldier is shot for desertion in 1962's *The Victors*. You will also hear Sinatra briefly in 1974's *Once Is Not Enough* singing "All The Way" (Van Heusen–Cahn), in 1976's *The Front* singing "Young At Heart" (Richards–Leigh), and also briefly in 1964's *Paris When It Sizzles*, 1981's *SOB*, and *They All Laughed*, and 1982's *Diner*.

It seems a safe bet that, were all the source music uses of big bands to be tallied, Glenn Miller And His Orchestra would come out one of the winners; probably more than any other of their recordings, the original "Moonlight Serenade" (Miller–Parish) perfectly recaptures the feel of the mid-1940s. It was uniquely featured in 1971's *Carnal Knowledge*, as well as in 1976's *Voyage Of The Damned* and 1980's *Stardust Memories*.

Stardust Memories is just one of Woody Allen's own pictures that is so perfectly punctuated with vintage jazz and popular music, drawn mainly from commercial recordings. His use of exclusively Gershwin music for *Manhattan* (1979) remains a masterpiece marriage of sound and vision. A similar exercise was attempted with the adaptation of Cole Porter melodies for the score of 1981's *Evil Under The Sun*.

In 1973, the television movie *Sunshine* featured the songs of singer-songwriter John Denver, including "Take Me Home, Country Roads" (Denver–Nivert–Danoff) and "Sunshine On My Shoulders" (Denver–Kniss–Taylor), though not Denver's own vocals. Two later motion pictures drew on the rich supply of two major artists' own recordings: 1976's *Alex And The Gypsy* featuring original tracks of jazz guitarist Django Reinhardt, and the soundtrack of 1977's *Semi-Tough* evoking the individual style of cowboy superstar Gene Autry.

The source music in 1970's *Five Easy Pieces* was derived from two diverse areas, namely the classical piano works of Chopin, Mozart and Bach, and four songs from the repertoire of country singer Tammy Wynette, including two of her biggest hits, "Stand By Your Man" (Sherill–Wynette) and "D-I-V-O-R-C-E" (Braddock–Putnam).

Of rock acts, The Bee Gees are among the groups used extensively, particularly following their *Saturday Night Fever* score in 1978, from which "Stayin' Alive" (B., M. and R. Gibb) is featured in 1978's *Foul Play*, 1980's *Airplane*, and 1980's *Neighbors*, while "Night Fever" (B., M. and R. Gibb) was heard in 1979's *Luna*.

The following is a random list of original commercial recordings which have been featured on the soundtracks of non-musical movies.

AC-CENT-TCHU-ATE THE POSITIVE (Arlen–Mercer)
Bing Crosby and The Andrews Sisters in *The Brink's Job* (1978)
ALL I HAVE TO DO IS DREAM (Bryant)

Juice Newton in *Shoot The Moon* (1981)

ALL OR NOTHING AT ALL (Altman–Lawrence)
Jimmy Dorsey And His Orchestra with Bob Eberly in *Missing* (1981)

BEHIND CLOSED DOORS (O'Dell)
Charlie Rich in *Every Which Way But Loose* (1978)

BIG GIRLS DON'T CRY (Crewe–Gaudio)
The Four Seasons in *The Main Event* (1979)

BIG NOISE FROM WINNETKA (Haggart – Crosby – Bauduc – Rodin)
Bob Crosby And The Bobcats in *Cannery Row* (1982)

BLUE MOON (Rodgers–Hart)
The Marcels, Sam Cooke, Bobby Vinton (all three individual versions), in *An American Werewolf In London* (1981)

COME RAIN OR COME SHINE (Arlen–Mercer)
Ray Charles in *The King Of Comedy* (1983)

DADDY (Troup)
The Andrews Sisters in *1941* (1979)

THE END (The Doors)
The Doors in *Apocalypse Now* (1979)

HELLO, I LOVE YOU (The Doors)
The Doors in *Neighbors* (1980)

HOW HIGH THE MOON (Lewis–Hamilton)
Les Paul And Mary Ford in *My Favorite Year* (1982)

I CAN'T GIVE YOU ANYTHING BUT LOVE, BABY (McHugh–Fields)

Rudy Vallee in *The Grissom Gang* (1971)

I FEEL THE EARTH MOVE (King)
Carole King in *Foul Play* (1978)
Carole King in *Slow Dancing In The Big City* (1978)

I HEARD IT THROUGH THE GRAPEVINE (Whitfield–Strong)
Marvin Gaye in *The Big Chill* (1983)

I LOVE THE NIGHT LIFE (Bridges–Hutcheson)
Alicia Bridges in *Love At First Bite* (1979)

I WANNA BE LOVED BY YOU (Kalmar–Stothart–Ruby)
Helen Kane in *Melvin Purvis, G-Man* (UK: *The Legend Of Machine Gun Kelly*) (1974)

I'LL BE SEEING YOU (Fain–Kahal)
Dinah Shore in *Fuzz* (1972)
Anne Shelton in *Yanks* (1979)
Billie Holiday in *Bad Timing* (1980)
(Also sung by film composer Fred Karlin in a non-commercial recording on the soundtrack of 1976's *Baby Blue Marine*.)

JEEPERS CREEPERS (Warren–Mercer)
Louis Armstrong (studio recording) in *Day Of The Locust* (1974)

LIGHT MY FIRE (The Doors)
The Doors in *Taps* (1981)

LOVE IS STRANGE (Baker–Robinson–Smith)
Mickey And Sylvia in *Badlands* (1973)

MEMORIES OF YOU (Blake–Razaf)
Benny Goodman And His Orchestra in *True Confessions* (1981)

MISTER SANDMAN (Ballard)
The Chordettes in *Halloween II* (1981)

(Also featured by an uncredited singer in *A Little Sex* (1982).)

OLD TIME ROCK AND ROLL (Jackson—Jones)
Bob Seger And The Silver Bullet Band in *Risky Business* (1983)

ON BROADWAY (Leiber—Stoller—Mann—Weil)
George Benson in *All That Jazz* (1979)

ON THE SUNNY SIDE OF THE STREET (McHugh—Fields)
Frankie Laine in *House Calls* (1978)
Willie Nelson in *Rich And Famous* (1981)

RIGHT BACK WHERE WE STARTED FROM (Tubbs—Edwards)
Maxine Nightingale in *Slap Shot* (1977)

RUBBERBAND MAN (Creed—Bell)
The Spinners in *Stripes* (1981)

SINCERELY (Fuqua—Freed)
The McGuire Sisters in *Come Back To The 5 & Dime, Jimmy Dean, Jimmy Dean* (1982)

SOMETHING (Harrison)
The Beatles in *House Calls* (1978)

SOMETHING IN THE AIR (Keen)
Thunderclap Newman in *The Magic Christian* (1970)
Thunderclap Newman in *The Strawberry Statement* (1970)

SOMETHING TO REMEMBER YOU BY (Schwartz—Dietz)
Helen Morgan in *The Telephone Book* (1971)
Helen Morgan in *A Safe Place* (1971)

STAR DUST (Parish—Carmichael)
Nat "King" Cole in *My Favorite Year* (1982)

TIP-TOE THROUGH THE TULIPS

WITH ME (Burke—Dubin)
Nick Lucas (studio recording) in *The Great Gatsby* (1974)

THE VERY THOUGHT OF YOU (Noble)
Nat "King" Cole in *Some Call It Loving* (1973)

WE'LL MEET AGAIN (Parker—Charles)
Vera Lynn, as Slim Pickens sits astride the H-bomb which is about to be dropped on Russia, in *Dr Strangelove, or How I Learned To Stop Worrying And Love The Bomb* (1964)

WHEN I'M SIXTY-FOUR (Lennon—McCartney)
The Beatles in *The World According To Garp* (1982)

YOU MAKE ME FEEL LIKE DANCING (Sayer)
Leo Sayer in *Slap Shot* (1977)

The velvet-voiced Nat "King" Cole was heard on the soundtracks of *Autumn Leaves* and *Raintree County*. He was also seen and heard on *Small Town Girl*, *China Gate*, *Istanbul* and *Cat Ballou*.

9 BORROWED TITLE SONGS

Recognisable song titles have often been recruited for the actual titles of movies, the producers obviously taking advantage of the public's automatic awareness of a hit phrase. Here are some examples:

AUTUMN LEAVES (Kosma–Prevert–Mercer)
Song originally based on a French ballad of the 1940s and sung in France by Juliette Greco. In 1950 the melody gave American pianist Roger Williams a best-selling record and, in 1956, it was sung by Nat "King" Cole on the soundtrack of the Joan Crawford movie of the same name.

BODY AND SOUL (Green–Heyman–Sour–Eyton)
First copyrighted in 1930, it was used as the theme for the 1947 John Garfield boxing movie *Body And Soul*. The 1981 remake retained the title but not the music.

BUT NOT FOR ME (Gershwin)
The Gershwin classic, first sung by Ginger Rogers in a 1930s musical show called *Girl Crazy*. Ella Fitzgerald sang it over the opening titles of the 1959 Clark Gable comedy also titled *But Not For Me*. (The film included another revival: Leroy Anderson's novelty instrumental, "The Typewriter", which Jerry Lewis performed so memorably in 1963's *Who's Minding The Store?*)

COME FLY WITH ME (Van Heusen–Cahn)
A song which first appeared as the title track of a Frank Sinatra album in 1958. A 1963 film about airline hostesses borrowed the title and commissioned Frankie Avalon (who did not appear in the film itself) to sing the song over the main titles.

I'LL BE SEEING YOU (Fain–Kahal)
Written in the 1930s, it became the title of a wartime love story in 1944, starring Ginger Rogers and Joseph Cotten. The song was sung by a studio chorus on the soundtrack.

JUST A GIGOLO (Casucci–Caesar)
A European song which was an American success in the 1930s. In 1979 a European production *Just A Gigolo* was shot with rock star David Bowie and the legendary Marlene Dietrich. Miss Dietrich sang the title song in her own inimitable style.

OUT OF NOWHERE (Green–Heyman)
This song was an early Bing Crosby favourite. Also known as "You Came Along (From Out Of Nowhere)", it provided the title of a Robert Cummings–Lizabeth Scott picture in 1945, *You Came Along*, in which it was sung on-screen by Helen Forrest.

SMILE (Chaplin–Turner–Parsons)
A song based on Charles Chaplin's theme from his 1936 *Modern Times* was a hit for Nat "King" Cole in 1954. The same Nat Cole recording was used on the soundtrack of 1975's *Smile*, the story of

BOTH LIVING A SECRET . . .

GINGER ROGERS
Challenging her "Kitty Foyle"

JOSEPH COTTEN
from his triumph in "Since You Went Away"

SHIRLEY TEMPLE
with grown-up glamour

EACH AFRAID TO TELL!

They came from different worlds, these two . . . living a
lie . . . fearing their past! The screen's newest romantic
pair . . . on the strangest holiday two people ever shared!

"I'LL BE SEEING YOU"

Directed by   Produced by
WILLIAM DIETERLE • DORE SCHARY
Screen Play by Marion Parsonnet
From a story by Charles Martin
A VANGUARD PRODUCTION—RELEASED THRU UNITED ARTISTS

"I'll Be Seeing You"
was written in the
1930s and became the
title of this 1944
movie.

a California beauty pageant.

WHO'LL STOP THE RAIN (Fogerty)
A 1970 hit for the group Cree-
dence Clearwater Revival. In
1978, Robert Stone's novel *Dog
Soldiers* was filmed and released
as *Who'll Stop The Rain*, featuring
the song on the soundtrack. Incidentally, in England where the

tune was unknown, the movie was released as *Dog Soldiers*.

YOU BROUGHT A NEW KIND OF LOVE TO ME (Fain–Kahal–Norman)
First sung by Maurice Chevalier in his 1930's *The Big Pond*. More than three decades later, part of the song's title was borrowed for a romantic comedy film, 1963's *A New Kind Of Love*, in which the original song was sung over the opening credits by Frank Sinatra.

This practice was also often adopted for a biographical film (biopics, as the industry refers to them) of composers and performers, which became known by songs already identified with the movie's subject.
Here are some examples:

THE BEST THINGS IN LIFE ARE FREE
The 1956 film on the lives of composers DeSylva, Brown and Henderson (with Gordon MacRae as DeSylva, Ernest Borgnine as Brown and Dan Dailey as Henderson).

I'LL SEE YOU IN MY DREAMS
The Gus Kahn story (Danny Thomas was Gus, Doris Day his wife) in 1951.

LOVE ME OR LEAVE ME
The Ruth Etting story (Doris Day was Ruth Etting) in 1955.

Rhapsody In Blue (1945), a musical biography, starred Robert Alda as George Gershwin and Paul Whiteman as himself.

NIGHT AND DAY

The Cole Porter story (Cary Grant was Cole Porter) in 1946.

RHAPSODY IN BLUE

The George Gershwin story (Robert Alda was Gershwin) in 1945.

ST. LOUIS BLUES

The W. C. Handy story (Nat "King" Cole was W. C. Handy and Billy Preston played Handy as a youngster) in 1958.

THREE LITTLE WORDS

The Kalmar and Ruby story (Fred Astaire was Bert Kalmar, Red Skelton was Harry Ruby) in 1950.

TILL THE CLOUDS ROLL BY

The Jerome Kern story (Robert Walker was Jerome Kern) in 1946.

WITH A SONG IN MY HEART

The Jane Froman story (Susan Hayward was Jane Froman) in 1952.

These are just a few of the many songs utilised as film titles over the years. Among the many others are: "If You Knew Susie", "Slaughter On Tenth Avenue", "It Had To Be You", "White Christmas", "Cruisin' Down The River", "Trail Of The Lonesome Pine", "Tea For Two" and "Beyond The Blue Horizon".

From time to time producers have also lifted movie titles from lyrics of popular songs, such as *Strawberry Blonde* from "The Band Played On" (Ward–Palmer) which became the constant theme of the 1941 James Cagney picture (you may recall the close of the film, when the song was reprised by a studio vocalist, with the lyric running across the screen, complete with a bouncing ball!). A more recent case of a similar title derivation was 1981's *Chariots Of Fire*, the phrase of which comes from the English hymn "Jerusalem" (Parry), sung on the soundtrack by The Ambrosian Singers.

An example of one song title being substituted for another occurred as this book was being completed. Willie Nelson's 1980 film, *Honeysuckle Rose*, contained the song "On The Road Again" (Nelson) which became a hit single for Nelson after the film's theatrical release. The picture initially played cable television under its original title, but was sold to an American network in 1982 as *On The Road Again*.

Other country music song titles, and in some cases, the lyrics themselves, have been developed as motion picture properties, including C. W. McCall's own "Convoy", Bobbie Gentry's composition "Ode To Billie Joe", the Jeannie C. Riley record "Harper Valley PTA" (Hall), Mary MacGregor's hit "Torn Between Two Lovers" (Yarrow–Yarrell), Vicki Lawrence's single "The Night The Lights Went Out in Georgia" (Russell), and the Johnny Paycheck anthem "Take This Job and Shove It" (Coe).

Of the previously published melodies incorporated into Hollywood scores, one of the most notable was "Moonglow" (Mills–DeLange–Hudson), written originally in the 1930s and integrated by George Duning into his score for 1956's *Picnic*. The official record label credit of the resultant theme read: "Moonglow and Theme From Picnic". Morris Stoloff — the film's musical director — had the big selling disc. Comedian–songwriter Steve Allen provided a lyric for the actual main theme and The McGuire

William Holden and Kim Novak dance together in *Picnic* (1956). The newly written theme was combined with the 1934 melody "Moonglow" which had been revived in the stage version of *Picnic*.

Sisters took that song into the best-sellers also.

From the 1920s "Together" (De-Sylva–Brown–Henderson) was revived in the score of the 1944 wartime drama, *Since You Went Away*, and "I'm Forever Blowing Bubbles" (Kenbrovin–Kellette) was not only the recurring theme of one of the premier gangster movies, 1931's *Public Enemy*, but also accompanied the main title sequence in 1969's *Women in Love*. Hoagy Carmichael's rendition of "Among My Souvenirs" (Nicholls–Leslie) in 1946's *The Best Years Of Our Lives* prompted a whole revival of the song's popularity during the film's release, with Frank Sinatra and Bing Crosby heading the list of artists who released new versions.

The 1982 MGM film *Shoot The Moon* used as its constant theme "Don't Blame Me" (McHugh–Fields) which had been featured in some earlier Metro pictures and was used as the promotional song for *Dinner At Eight* in 1933. It is played on the soundtrack primarily by single piano notes, and is sung in a restaurant scene by Helen Slayton-Hughes. By the way, one of the film's stars, Diane Keaton, sings a few lines from "If I Fell" (Lennon–McCartney) in the same movie.

"You'll Never Know" (Warren–Gordon) was used as the recurring romantic theme in 1956's *D-Day, The Sixth Of June*, and "These Foolish Things (Remind Me of You)" (Strachey–Link–Marvell) played a similar role in 1941's *A Yank In The RAF*. Obviously these are but a few of the countless occasions when standard tunes have been revived in movies; sometimes they don't exactly fit the context of the storyline, as in 1946's *Young Widow*, when "(All of a Sudden) My Heart Sings" (Rome) is used in flashback scenes for a period pre-dating the actual song.

Finally, three songs which were each revived for a main title sequence and sung by the respective studio choruses: "Remember Me" (Warren–Dubin) in 1946's *Never Say Goodbye*, "Pretty Baby" (Alstyne–Jackson–Kahn) in 1948's *Sitting Pretty*, and "I'm in the Mood for Love" in 1959's *Ask Any Girl*. Though it was played rather than sung, "Make 'Em Laugh" (Brown–Freed) accompanied the opening visuals in 1975's *The Sunshine Boys* and, similarly, Cole Porter's "Anything Goes" provided the perfect musical introduction to 1970's *Boys In The Band*.

The 1937 sheet (showing tenor Kenny Baker) for the song used in 1946's *Never Say Goodbye*, and more recently revived on stage by Shirley MacLaine.

10 THE SONG ABOVE THE TITLE

There are no rules as to where songs appear in motion pictures — whether they are sung for narrative purposes, performed at the opening and/or closing of a movie, or simply created as a promotional aid to the picture's publicity campaign.

Silent movies had been provided with specially composed scores for the pit musicians to play and the best example of a lasting melody emerging from such a work is "Charmaine" (Rapee–Pollock), written for the 1926 production *What Price Glory*.

Quite by chance, an orchestral recording of the same tune by British conductor Mantovani became a best-selling record in 1951, and when 20th Century-Fox remade *What Price*

Nancy Carroll sang this theme song in the 1928 part-talkie *The Shopworn Angel*, starring Gary Cooper.

Glory the following year, "Charmaine" was incorporated in the soundtrack music.

1927's *The Jazz Singer* with its famed musical sequences is generally regarded as marking the official commencement of sound movies. In the year that followed, Nancy Carroll sang one of the first songs in a non-musical, namely "A Precious Little Thing Called Love" (Coots–Davis) in the part-talkie *The Shopworn Angel*. At the same time, the legendary Fanny Brice gave forth one of the first movie title songs, "My Man" (Yvain–Pollock), though the song was not original either to the film or its star, as Miss Brice had introduced it on Broadway in the *Ziegfeld Follies Of 1921*. 1928 also witnessed the popularity of the song "Ramona" (Wayne–Gilbert), the first song to be "inspired" by a motion picture (a category discussed in a later chapter) in that the film itself was silent and the song was sung by its star, Dolores del Rio, on promotional appearances.

So movie title songs (those based on the main theme, often bearing the same title as the picture, and usually featured over the credit titles) have been with us for some considerable time. They became particularly fashionable after 1952, the year in which Tex Ritter's voice singing the Dimitri Tiomkin–Ned Washington song "High Noon" (subtitled "Do Not Forsake Me") opened and closed the Gary Cooper western.

A number of other pictures in the same genre followed this lead, and rich-voiced Frankie Laine (who, ironically, had enjoyed more success on record with the "High Noon" song than Ritter himself) was hired to sing over the titles of a whole series of films; apart from those included in our list below, Frankie Laine also sang the title songs in 1955's *Man Without A Star* (Hughes–Herbert), 1955's *Strange Lady In Town* (Tiomkin–Washington), 1957's *3.10 To Yuma* (Duning–Washington) and, most recently, 1974's *Blazing Saddles* (Morris–Brooks).

Virtually every major singer of the past three decades has sung on the soundtrack of one or more movies, and a comprehensive list of title songs would require more space than we have here at present. Two oddities are worth mentioning in passing: in one of the strangest combinations of talents in the recording of a title song, 1966's "After The Fox", written for the Peter Sellers comedy by Burt Bach-

arach and Hal David, was performed by Mr Sellers together with pop stars The Hollies; and, in 1971, when Charles Chaplin was preparing the reissue of his 1928 silent comedy *The Circus*, he not only wrote the musical score, but also a title song which he himself, at the age of 82, sang.

Above: Frankie Laine sang over the titles for a series of films in the 1950s.

Left: Dolores del Rio sang "Ramona" during promotional appearances for the film of the same name.

11 MOVIE TITLE SONGS

The following is a selected list of movie title songs indicating, where applicable, the relevant recording artists who popularised each composition, other than those who sang on the soundtracks.

AN AFFAIR TO REMEMBER (OUR LOVE AFFAIR) (Warren–Adamson–McCarey)
Vic Damone in *An Affair To Remember* (1957)
ALFIE (Bacharach–David)
Cher in *Alfie* (1966)
(See "Inspired Movie Songs".)
(Also a hit for Dionne Warwick (US) and Cilla Black (UK).)
ALL THE RIGHT MOVES (Snow–Alfonso)
Jennifer Warnes and Chris Thompson in *All The Right Moves* (1983)
ANY WHICH WAY YOU CAN (Brown–Dorff–Garrett)
Glen Campbell in *Any Which Way You Can* (1980)
THE APRIL FOOLS (Bacharach–David)
Dionne Warwick in *The April Fools* (1969)
ARTHUR'S THEME (BEST THAT YOU CAN DO) (Bacharach–Sager–Cross–Allen)
Christopher Cross in *Arthur* (1980)

BEN (Scharf–Black)
Michael Jackson in *Ben* (1972)
THE BEST OF EVERYTHING (Newman–Cahn)
Johnny Mathis in *The Best Of Everything* (1959)
BLOWING WILD (THE BALLAD OF BLACK GOLD) (Tiomkin–Washington)
Frankie Laine in *Blowing Wild* (1953)
BORN FREE (Barry–Black)
Matt Monro in *Born Free* (1965)
(Not heard on the soundtrack of the original British release of the film, though it won the Best Song Oscar.)
BREATHLESS (Blackwell)
X and also by Jerry Lee Lewis in *Breathless* (1983)

CAT PEOPLE (PUTTING OUT FIRE) (Moroder–Bowie)
David Bowie in *Cat People* (1982)
A CERTAIN SMILE (Fain–Webster)
Johnny Mathis in *A Certain Smile* (1958)
CHARADE (Mancini–Mercer)
Studio Chorus in *Charade* (1963)
(Hit records by Andy Williams and Henry Mancini.)
Theme from CLEOPATRA JONES (Simon)
Joe Simon and Millie Jackson in *Cleopatra Jones* (1973)

Ballad of DAVY CROCKETT (Blackburn–Bruns)
(Originally written for and introduced on the soundtrack of the television series *Disneyland* (1954).
Fess Parker in *Davy Crockett, King Of The Wild Frontier!* (1955)
Also featured in *Davy Crockett And The River Pirates* (1957)
(Parker himself had one of the major hit records of the song, with Bill Hayes's version reaching the highest chart position.)

THE DAYS OF WINE AND ROSES (Mancini–Mercer)
Studio Chorus in *The Days Of Wine And Roses* (1962)
(Hit recordings by Andy Williams and Henry Mancini.)

DEAR HEART (Mancini–Livingston–Evans)
Studio Chorus in *Dear Heart* (1964)
(Hit recordings by Andy Williams, Jack Jones and Henry Mancini.)

Theme from THE DEEP (DOWN, DEEP INSIDE) (Barry–Summer)
Donna Summer in *The Deep* (1977)

EASY MONEY (Joel)
Billy Joel in *Easy Money* (1983)

ENDLESS LOVE (Richie)
Diana Ross and Lionel Richie in *Endless Love* (1981)

EVERY WHICH WAY BUT LOOSE (Dorff–Brown–Garrett)
Eddie Rabbitt in *Every Which Way But Loose* (1978)

FIRE DOWN BELOW (Lee–Washington)
Jeri Southern in *Fire Down Below* (1957)

FLASHDANCE — WHAT A FEELING (Forsey–Cara)
Irene Cara in *Flashdance* (1983)

FRIENDLY PERSUASION (THEE I LOVE) (Tiomkin–Webster)
Pat Boone in *Friendly Persuasion* (1956)

GEORGY GIRL (Springfield–Dale)
The Seekers in *Georgy Girl* (1966)

GIANT (Tiomkin — Webster)
Studio Chorus, on the fadeout of *Giant* (1956)
(Orchestra leader Les Baxter had the biggest record success.)

GIDGET (Karger–Washington)
James Darren in *Gidget* (1959)

GOODBYE, COLUMBUS (Yester)
The Association in *Goodbye, Columbus* (1969)

GOODBYE GIRL (Gates)
David Gates in *The Goodbye Girl* (1977)

GREASE (Barry Gibb)
Frankie Valli in *Grease* (1978)
(Title song of the musical, although not a musical number itself; sung over the movie credits.)

GUNFIGHT AT THE O.K. CORRAL (Tiomkin–Washington)
Frankie Laine in *Gunfight At The O.K. Corral* (1957)

THE HANGING TREE (Livingston–David)
Marty Robbins in *The Hanging Tree* (1959)

THE HAPPENING (De Vol–Roy)
The Supremes in *The Happening* (1967)

A HARD DAY'S NIGHT (Lennon–McCartney)
The Beatles in *A Hard Day's Night* (1964)
(Hit songs by The Beatles were given to all four of their own films, namely their two musicals, *A Hard Day's Night* and *Help!*, the semi-documentary *Let It Be*, and the animated feature *Yellow Submarine*.)

THE HIGH AND THE MIGHTY (Tiomkin–Washington)
Studio Chorus in *The High And The Mighty* (1954)
(Melody was originally whistled, rather than sung, on the soundtrack; however, a vocal version was inserted when the Academy announced the song would not otherwise be eligible for an Oscar nomination.)

Right: The melody in *The High And The Mighty* (1954) was originally whistled, but a vocal version was inserted on the soundtrack to qualify it for an Academy Award nomination.

Far right: "Do Not Forsake Me" opened and closed *High Noon*, starring Gary Cooper and Grace Kelly.

Singing cowboy Tex Ritter is perhaps best remembered for performing the narrative song in *High Noon* (1952). It prompted Capitol Records to release his album, "Songs From The Western Screen".

HIGH NOON (DO NOT FORSAKE ME) (Tiomkin–Washington)
Tex Ritter in *High Noon* (1952)
(Also a major hit song for Frankie Laine.)

HIGH SCHOOL CONFIDENTIAL Lewis–Hargrove)
Jerry Lee Lewis in *High School Confidential* (1958)
(At the opening of the movie, Jerry Lee is seen rocking the title song from the back of a truck!)

HONKYTONK MAN (Blackwell)
Marty Robbins in *Honkytonk Man* (1982)

HOT STUFF (Reed)
Jerry Reed in *Hot Stuff* (1979)

Love song from HOUSEBOAT (ALMOST IN YOUR ARMS) (Livingston–Evans)
Sam Cooke in *Houseboat* (1958)

HUSH, HUSH, SWEET CHARLOTTE (De Vol–David)
Al Martino in *Hush, Hush, Sweet Charlotte* (1964)

Doris Day on a promotional stint for the title song from her picture *Julie* (1956). With her is Hollywood disc-jockey Johnny Grant.

IF A MAN ANSWERS (Darin)
Bobby Darin in *If A Man Answers* (1962)

IF IT'S TUESDAY, THIS MUST BE BELGIUM (Leitch)
Donovan in *If It's Tuesday This Must Be Belgium* (1969)

IN THE HEAT OF THE NIGHT (Jones–A. and M. Bergman)
Ray Charles in *In The Heat Of The Night* (1967)

INTERLUDE (Delerue–Shaper)
Timi Yuro in *Interlude* (1968)

(Not to be confused with the title song from the similarly titled 1957 film, sung by The McGuire Sisters.)

ISLAND IN THE SUN (Belafonte–Burgess)
Harry Belafonte in *Island In The Sun* (1957)

IT'S A MAD, MAD, MAD, MAD WORLD (Gold–David)
Studio Chorus in *It's A Mad, Mad, Mad, Mad World* (1973)
(A hit song for The Shirelles.)

IT'S MY TURN (Masser–Sayer)
Diana Ross in *It's My Turn* (1980)

JEAN (McKuen)
Rod McKuen in *The Prime Of Miss Jean Brodie* (1969)

JOE HILL (Robinson–Hayes)
Joan Baez in *Joe Hill* (1971)

JOHNNY GUITAR (Young–Lee)
Peggy Lee in *Johnny Guitar* (1953)

JULIE (Stevens–Adair)
Doris Day in *Julie* (1956)

KATHY O' (Sher–Tobias–Joseph)
The Diamonds in *Kathy O'* (1958)

THE LEGEND OF CHUCK-A-LUCK (Davey)
William Lee in *Rancho Notorious* (1952)
(Sung periodically throughout the film as an ongoing narrative.)

LET'S DO IT AGAIN (Mayfield)
The Staple Singers in *Let's Do It Again* (1975)

The Ballad of LITTLE FAUSS AND BIG HALSY (Perkins)
Johnny Cash in *Little Fauss And Big Halsy* (1970)

THE LONG HOT SUMMER (North–Cahn)
Jimmie Rodgers in *The Long Hot Summer* (1958)

LOVE IS A MANY-SPLENDORED THING (Fain–Webster)
Studio Chorus in *Love Is A Many-Splendored Thing* (1955)
(The Four Aces had the biggest hit with this song and their recording was used on the soundtrack of 1979's *Heartbeat*. An orchestral version of the main theme was also briefly heard in 1978's *Grease*.)

LOVE ME TENDER (Matson–Presley)
Elvis Presley in *Love Me Tender* (1956)

(Adapted from a Civil War melody "Aura Lee", "Love Me Tender" was co-written by Elvis with Vera Matson, wife of composer–arranger Ken Darby. The film itself was Presley's first musical, with Elvis performing the song in an early sequence.)

LOVE WITH THE PROPER STRANGER (Bernstein–Schulman)
Jack Jones in *Love With The Proper Stranger* (1963)

Theme from MAHOGANY (DO YOU KNOW WHERE YOU'RE GOING TO) (Masser–Goffin)
Diana Ross in *Mahogany* (1975)

THE MAIN EVENT (Jabara–Roberts)
Barbra Streisand in *The Main Event* (1979)

MAKING LOVE (Bacharach–Sayer–Roberts)
Roberta Flack in *Making Love* (1982)

THE MAN FROM LARAMIE (Lee–Washington)
Studio Chorus in *The Man From Laramie* (1955)
(Various hit recordings, including The Voices Of Walter Schumann, and in England, Jimmy Young.)

MAYBE (Bacharach–Sager–Hamlisch)
Peabo Bryson and Roberta Flack in *Romantic Comedy* (1983)

THE MONKEY'S UNCLE (R. B. and R. M. Sherman)
Annette (Funicello) and The Beach Boys in *The Monkey's Uncle* (1965)
(For this, The Beach Boys belong to a select group of major singing acts who have performed a movie's title song during the opening titles sequence, while not appearing in the film itself. Sheena Easton, singing "For Your Eyes Only", is a more recent example.)

Dana Andrews and
Susan Hayward in
My Foolish Heart
(1950). Martha Mears
(in the spotlight at the
back of the room)
sang the title song.

Melina Mercouri per-
forms to the strains
of Hadjidakis's song
"Never on Sunday"
in the 1960 picture of
the same name.

THE MOON IS BLUE (Gilbert–Fine)
Studio Chorus in *The Moon Is Blue* (1953)

MORE (Ortolani–Newell)
Kathine Ortolani in *Mondo Cane* (1963)
(Song actually only heard in the American release, having been written after the film's initial Italian success, by British record producer, Norman Newell.)

MOVE OVER DARLING (Melcher–Lubin–Kanter)
Doris Day in *Move Over Darling* (1963)

MY FOOLISH HEART (Young–Washington)
Martha Mears in *My Foolish Heart* (1949)
(The biggest record sellers in the States were Billy Eckstine and Gordon Jenkins And His Orchestra, and the most popular version in the UK was by the late Steve Conway.)

NEVER ON SUNDAY (Hadjidakis)
Melina Mercouri, in Greek, in *Never On Sunday* (1960)
(With an English lyric by Bob Towne, the song was recorded extensively, but primarily is remembered as having charted for both The Chordettes, and the late Don Costa.)

NINE TO FIVE (Parton)
Dolly Parton in *9 To 5* (1980)

NORTH TO ALASKA (Phillips)
Johnny Horton in *North To Alaska* (1960)

ON A CLEAR DAY YOU CAN SEE FOREVER (Lane–Lerner)
Barbra Streisand and Yves Montand sang this in the 1970 film version of the musical show *On A Clear Day You Can See Forever*. The song has far outlived the movie, and was most successfully recorded by Johnny Mathis.

PIECES OF DREAMS (Legrand–M. and A. Bergman)
Peggy Lee in *Pieces Of Dreams* (1970)

POCKET MONEY (King)
Carole King in *Pocket Money* (1972)

POCKETFUL OF MIRACLES (Van Heusen–Cahn)
Frank Sinatra in *Pocketful Of Miracles* (1961)

The Song of RAINTREE COUNTY (Green–Webster)
Nat "King" Cole in *Raintree County* (1957)

RETURN TO PARADISE (Tiomkin–Washington)
Kitty White in *Return To Paradise* (1953)

RIDE THE WILD SURF (Berry–Wilson–Christian)

Peggy Lee sang the title song in *Pieces Of Dreams* (1970).

Jan And Dean in *Ride The Wild Surf* (1964)
RIO BRAVO (Tiomkin–Webster)
    Dean Martin in *Rio Bravo* (1959)
RIVER OF NO RETURN (Newman–Darby)
    Marilyn Monroe and Tennessee Ernie Ford in *River Of No Return* (1954)

SAYONARA (Berlin)
    Studio Chorus in *Sayonara* (1957)
THE SEARCHERS (RIDE AWAY) (Jones)
    The Sons of the Pioneers in *The Searchers* (1956)
Theme from SHAFT (Hayes)
    Isaac Hayes in *Shaft* (1971)
SLAUGHTER (Preston)
    Billy Preston in *Slaughter* (1972)
SOLDIER BLUE (Sainte-Marie)
    Buffy Sainte-Marie in *Soldier Blue* (1970)
SOMEBODY UP THERE LIKES ME (Kaper–Cahn)
    Perry Como in *Somebody Up There Likes Me* (1956)
SUNDAY IN NEW YORK (Nero–Gates)
    Mel Torme in *Sunday In New York* (1964)
SUPERFLY (Mayfield)
    Curtis Mayfield in *Superfly* (1972)
TAMMY (Livingston–Evans)
    The Ames Brothers in *Tammy And The Bachelor* (UK: *Tammy*) (1957) (See also "The Singers and the Songs in Non-Musicals".)
TENDER IS THE NIGHT (Fain–Webster)
    Earl Grant in *Tender Is The Night* (1961)
(Love Is) THE TENDER TRAP (Van Heusen–Cahn)
    Frank Sinatra in *The Tender Trap* (1955)
THANK GOD IT'S FRIDAY (Costan-

didos)
    Love And Kisses in *Thank God It's Friday* (1978)
THOSE MAGNIFICENT MEN IN THEIR FLYING MACHINES (Goodwin)
    Studio Chorus in *Those Magnificent Men In Their Flying Machines* (1965)
THREE COINS IN THE FOUNTAIN (Styne–Cahn)
    Frank Sinatra in *Three Coins In The Fountain* (1954)
The Ballad of THUNDER ROAD (Raye–Mitchum)
    Keely Smith in *Thunder Road*

Keely Smith sings the title song in *Thunder Road* (1958). Robert Mitchum recorded it commercially and it became a big seller.

Jack Jones popular-
ised "Where Love
Has Gone" from the
1964 picture of the
same title.

(1958)
(Recorded commercially by
Robert Mitchum and a subsequent
hit.)
TO SIR, WITH LOVE (London–Black)
Lulu in *To Sir, With Love* (1967)
(Actually sung by Lulu on-screen
in the film.)
TONY ROME (May-Hazlewood)
Nancy Sinatra in *Tony Rome*
(1967)
TOWN WITHOUT PITY (Tiomkin–
Washington)
Gene Pitney in *Town Without
Pity* (1961)
TROUBLE MAN (Gaye)
Marvin Gaye in *Trouble Man*
(1972)
TRUE GRIT (Bernstein–Black)
Glen Campbell in *True Grit* (1969)

UNCHAINED MELODY (Lonely
River) (North–Zareth)
Todd Duncan in *Unchained* (1955)
UNFAITHFULLY YOURS (ONE
LOVE) (Bishop)
Stephen Bishop in *Unfaithfully
Yours* (1984)

Theme from VALLEY OF THE DOLLS
(Andre and Dory Previn)
Dionne Warwick in *Valley Of The
Dolls* (1967)

WALK ON THE WILD SIDE (Bern-
stein–David)
Brook Benton in *Walk On The
Wild Side* (1961)
Ballad of THE WAR WAGON
(Tiomkin–Washington)
Ed Ames in *The War Wagon*
(1967)
THE WAY WE WERE (Hamlisch–
A. and M. Bergman)
Barbra Streisand in *The Way We
Were* (1974)
WHAT'S NEW PUSSYCAT? (Bach-
arach–David)
Tom Jones in *What's New
Pussycat* (1965)
(Song also featured in the long
forgotten 1970 sequel, *Pussycat,
Pussycat, I Love You*; Burt
Bacharach's own recording of the
song featured a vocal by Joel
Grey.)
WHERE LOVE HAS GONE (Van
Heusen–Cahn)
Jack Jones in *Where Love Has
Gone* (1964)
WHERE THE BOYS ARE (Sedaka–
Greenfield)
Connie Francis in *Where The Boys
Are* (1960)

WILD IN THE COUNTRY (Peretti–
    Creatore–Weiss)
    Elvis Presley in *Wild In The
    Country* (1961)
    (Title song from another Presley
    musical, his seventh film.)
WILD IS THE WIND (Tiomkin–
    Washington)
    Johnny Mathis in *Wild Is The
    Wind* (1957)
WRITTEN ON THE WIND (Young–
    Cahn)
    The Four Aces in *Written On The
    Wind* (1956)

YOUR PLACE OR MINE (Man-
    chester–Willis–Bryant)
    Melissa Manchester in *A Little Sex*
    (1982)

Advertisement for the original version of *Where The Boys Are* (MGM: 1960) in which Connie Francis sang the title song over the opening credits.

12 BOND-ED TITLE SONGS

The series of James Bond films which began with *Dr No* in 1962 has fashioned its own tradition of title songs. *Dr No* itself had no title song as such, but it did introduce the guitar-dominated "James Bond Theme" (written by Monty Norman), which became 007's identifiable melody in all the subsequent pictures.

The composer most associated with the Bond films, John Barry, separately recorded the "James Bond Theme" with his own instrumental group, The John Barry Seven, providing the very first Bond hit in England in late 1962.

The Bond title songs began with the second film in the series:

FROM RUSSIA WITH LOVE (Bart)
   sung by Matt Monro on the soundtrack in *From Russia With Love* (1963)

GOLDFINGER (Barry–Bricusse–Newley)

The "James Bond Theme", separately recorded by The John Barry Seven, was the first Bond hit in England in 1962.

Shirley Bassey in *Goldfinger* (1964)

THUNDERBALL (Barry–Black)
   Tom Jones in *Thunderball* (1965)

YOU ONLY LIVE TWICE (Barry–Bricusse)
   Nancy Sinatra in *You Only Live Twice* (1968)

WE HAVE ALL THE TIME IN THE WORLD (Barry–David)
   Louis Armstrong in *On Her Majesty's Secret Service* (1969)

DIAMONDS ARE FOREVER (Barry–Black)
   Shirley Bassey in *Diamonds Are Forever* (1971)

LIVE AND LET DIE (P. and L. McCartney)
   Paul McCartney And Wings in *Live And Let Die* (1973)

THE MAN WITH THE GOLDEN GUN (Barry–Black)
   Lulu in *The Man With The Golden Gun* (1974)

NOBODY DOES IT BETTER (Hamlisch–Sager)
   Carly Simon in *The Spy Who Loved Me* (1977)

MOONRAKER (Barry–David)
   Shirley Bassey in *Moonraker* (1979)

FOR YOUR EYES ONLY (Conti–Leeson)
   Sheena Easton in *For Your Eyes Only* (1981)

ALL TIME HIGH (Barry–Rice)
   Rita Coolidge in *Octopussy* (1983)

Of these singers, only Sheena Easton

was actually visible on the screen, her performance being incorporated in the main title sequence in *For Your Eyes Only*. In addition, the title song from *Live And Let Die* was also performed on-screen by B. J. (Brenda) Arnau.

There were however, three other James Bond hits. In 1967 a spoof on the character was released (through different producers) under the title *Casino Royale*. The film was scored by Burt Bacharach (Herb Alpert charted with the theme) and it included the ballad "The Look Of Love" (Bacharach–David) sung on the soundtrack by Dusty Springfield.

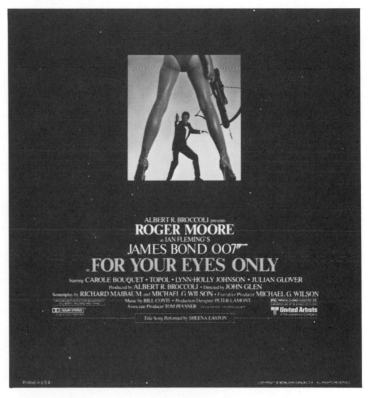

ALBERT R. BROCCOLI presents
ROGER MOORE
as IAN FLEMING'S
JAMES BOND 007
in FOR YOUR EYES ONLY
Starring CAROLE BOUQUET · TOPOL · LYNN-HOLLY JOHNSON · JULIAN GLOVER
Produced by ALBERT R. BROCCOLI · Directed by JOHN GLEN
Screenplay by RICHARD MAIBAUM and MICHAEL G WILSON · Executive Producer MICHAEL G. WILSON
Music by BILL CONTI · Production Designer PETER LAMONT
Associate Producer TOM PEVSNER
United Artists
Title Song Performed by SHEENA EASTON

Herb Alpert also played trumpet on the recording of the title song to the second Bond film of 1983, *Never Say Never Again* (Legrand–A. and M. Bergman), which was sung by Lani Hall (alias Mrs Alpert).

Of all the singers in the James Bond movies, only Sheena Easton was visible on the screen when she sang the title song in *For Your Eyes Only* (1981).

Louis Armstrong at the recording session of "We Have All The Time In The World", from *On Her Majesty's Secret Service* (1969).

13 MOVIE THEME SONGS

This section is devoted to key compositions, other than specific title songs, which have played significant roles on film soundtracks. In the majority of cases, these songs were specially commissioned by the producers.

AL DI LA (Donida–Mogo–Drake)
> Emilio Pericoli in *Rome Adventure* (UK: *Lovers Must Learn*) (1962)
> (Not written for, but used to great effect in the film; it won the San Remo Song Festival in Italy the previous year.)

ARE YOU MAN ENOUGH? (Lambert–Potter)
> The Four Tops in *Shaft In Africa* (1973)

BAR ROOM BUDDIES (Brown–Crofford–Dorff–Garrett)
> Merle Haggard and Clint Eastwood in *Bronco Billy* (1980)

BE (Diamond)
> Neil Diamond in *Jonathan Livingston Seagull* (1973)

BORN TO BE WILD (Bonfire)
> Steppenwolf in *Easy Rider* (1969)
> (A milestone in youth cinema. Probably, after "Rock Around

Angie Dickinson and Troy Donahue in *Rome Adventure* (1962), released in the UK as *Lovers Must Learn*. Emilio Pericoli sang the international hit, "Al Di La".

The Clock" in *Blackboard Jungle*, the foremost thematic use of a rock song on a soundtrack.)

BRIGHT EYES (Batt)
Art Garfunkel in *Watership Down* (1978)

BURNING BRIDGES (Schifrin–Curb)
The Mike Curb Congregation in *Kelly's Heroes* (1970)

CALL ME (Moroder–Harry)
Blondie in *American Gigolo* (1980) (The same recording featured on the soundtrack of 1982's *Partners*.)

CAN YOU READ MY MIND (Williams–Bricusse)
Margot Kidder in *Superman* (1978) (Maureen McGovern had the hit.)

CARRY ON WAYWARD SON (Livgren)
Kansas in *Heroes* (1977)

CHRISTMAS DREAM (Webber–Rice–Heller)
Perry Como in *The Odessa File* (1974)

COME AND GET IT (McCartney)
Badfinger in *The Magic Christian* (1970)

COME SATURDAY MORNING (Karlin–Previn)
The Sandpipers in *The Sterile Cuckoo* (UK: *Pookie*) (1970)

COME TO ME (Mancini–Black)
Tom Jones, along with a brief solo by Peter Sellers in the voice of Inspector Clouseau, in *The Pink Panther Strikes Again* (1976)

COULD I HAVE THIS DANCE (Holyfield–House)
Anne Murray in *Urban Cowboy* (1980)

COULD IT BE MAGIC (Manilow–Anderson)
Barry Manilow, Donna Summer and Adrienne Anderson in *Looking For Mr Goodbar* (1977)

DARLING, BE HOME SOON (Sebastian)
The Lovin' Spoonful in *You're A Big Boy Now* (1967)

DAYBREAK (Nilsson)
Harry Nilsson in *Son Of Dracula* (1974)
(Nilsson's earlier hit "Without You" featured in the same film.)

DON'T ASK TO STAY UNTIL TOMORROW (Kane–Connors)
Marlena Shaw in *Looking For Mr Goodbar* (1977)

(DON'T FEAR) THE REAPER (Roeser)
Blue Oyster Cult in *Halloween* (1978)

EAST BOUND AND DOWN (Feller–Reed)

Singer-songwriter Fred Neil's composition, "Everybody's Talkin'", which he recorded in 1967, was re-cut by Harry Nilsson for the soundtrack of *Midnight Cowboy* (1969). (Album cover by courtesy of Capitol/EMI Records.)

Jerry Reed in *Smokey And The Bandit* (1977)

EVERYBODY'S TALKIN' (Neil)
Harry Nilsson in *Midnight Cowboy* (1969)

EYE OF THE TIGER (Sullivan–Peterik)
Survivor in *Rocky III* (1982)

FEEL LIKE A NUMBER (Seger)
Bob Seger And The Silver Bullet Band in *Body Heat* (1981)

FOR ALL WE KNOW (Karlin–James–Wilson)
Larry Meredith in *Lovers And Other Strangers* (1969)
(Co-composers Arthur James and Robb Wilson are pseudonyms for members of the group, Bread.)

FORGET DOMANI (Ortolani–Newell)
Katyna Ranieri in *The Yellow Rolls-Royce* (1965)

The music became very successful after *Rocky* (1976) won the Best Picture Oscar in 1977. (Album cover by courtesy of MGM/UA and EMI Records.)

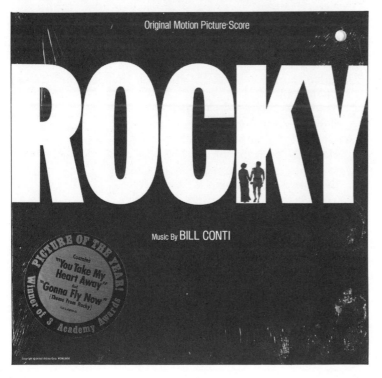

Original Motion Picture Score

ROCKY

Music By BILL CONTI

(Both Frank Sinatra and Connie Francis had best-selling versions.)

FREDDIE'S DEAD (Theme from *Superfly*) (Mayfield)
Curtis Mayfield in *Superfly* (1972)

FRIENDS (Klingman–Linhart)
Bette Midler in *The Last Of Sheila* (1973)

GIVE ME THAT OLD TIME RELIGION (Traditional)
Leslie Uggams in *Inherit The Wind* (1960)

GONNA FLY NOW (Theme from *Rocky*) (Conti–Connors–Robbins)
Bill Conti in *Rocky* (1976)
(The first *Rocky* theme — written, arranged and conducted by Conti, who had the biggest record success, followed closely by Maynard Ferguson.)

THE GREATEST LOVE OF ALL (Masser–Goffin)
George Benson in *The Greatest* (1977)

HE GIVES US ALL HIS LOVE (Newman)
Randy Newman in *Cold Turkey* (1970)

HELP ME MAKE IT THROUGH THE NIGHT (Kristofferson)
Kris Kristofferson in *Fat City* (1972)

HOLD MY HAND (Lawrence–Myers)
Don Cornell in *Susan Slept Here* (1954)

HOW DO YOU KEEP THE MUSIC PLAYING (Legrand–A. and M. Bergman)
Patti Austin and James Ingram in *Best Friends* (1982)

I DON'T NEED YOU ANYMORE (Bacharach–Anka)
Jackie DeShannon in *Together?* (1979)

I GOT A NAME (Fox–Gimbel)
Jim Croce in *The Last American Hero* (1973)

I HAVE BUT ONE HEART (Farrow–Symes)
Al Martino in *The Godfather* (1972)

I HEAR A RHAPSODY (Fragos–Gasparre–Baker)
Tony Martin in *Clash By Night* (1952)

I NEED A LOVER (Mellencamp)
John Cougar in *Private Lessons* (1980)

I'M EASY (Loggins)
Kenny Loggins in *Caddyshack* (1980)

I'M ON YOUR SIDE (Hamlisch–Sager)
Marilyn McCoo in *Chapter Two* (1979)

ISTANBUL BLUES (Castle)
David Castle in *Midnight Express* (1978)

IT GOES LIKE IT GOES (Shire–Gimbel)
Melissa Manchester in *Norma Rae* (1979)

IT MIGHT BE YOU (Grusin–A. and M. Bergman)
Stephen Bishop in *Tootsie* (1982)

KNOCKIN' ON HEAVEN'S DOOR (Dylan)
Bob Dylan in *Pat Garrett And Billy The Kid* (1973)

THE LAST TIME I FELT LIKE THIS (Hamlisch–A. and M. Bergman)
Johnny Mathis and Jane Olivor in *Same Time, Next Year* (1978)

THE LAST TIME I SAW PARIS (Kern–Hammerstein)
Odette in *The Last Time I Saw Paris* (1954)
(Sung throughout the film, but not over the main or closing titles; song originally winner of Best Song Oscar in 1941, when it was sung by Ann Sothern in the MGM musical *Lady Be Good*.)

LITTLE BOYS (Mancini–A. and M. Bergman)
Helen Reddy in *The Man Who Loved Women* (1983)

LOOK WHAT YOU'VE DONE TO ME (Scaggs–Foster)
Boz Scaggs in *Urban Cowboy* (1980)

LOOKIN' FOR LOVE (Mallette–Ryan–Morrison)
Johnny Lee in *Urban Cowboy* (1980)

LOVE THE WORLD AWAY (Morrison–Wilson)
Kenny Rogers in *Urban Cowboy* (1980)

LOVE WILL TURN YOU AROUND (Rogers – Stevens – Schyler – Malloy)
Kenny Rogers in *Six Pack* (1982)

MAKIN' IT (Perren–Fekaris)
David Naughton in *Meatballs* (1979)
(Also a chart-making television theme song.)

MANIAC (Sembello–Matkosky)
Michael Sembello in *Flashdance* (1983)

MRS ROBINSON (Simon)
Simon And Garfunkel in *The Graduate* (1967)
(A standout set of Simon And Garfunkel tracks produced an unforgettable soundtrack, also including "Scarborough Fair/Canticle", and "The Sound Of Silence".)

THE MORNING AFTER (Song from THE POSEIDON ADVENTURE) (Kasha–Hirschhorn)
Maureen McGovern in *The Poseidon Adventure* (1972)

MY FAIR SHARE (Love Theme from

Paul Williams sang his own lyric, "Nice To Be Around", to John Williams' main theme in *Cinderella Liberty* (1973) starring James Caan and Marsha Mason.

ONE ON ONE) (Fox–Williams)
Seals And Croft in *One On One* (1977)

NICE TO BE AROUND (J. and P. Williams)
Paul Williams in *Cinderella Liberty* (1973)

ON AND ON (Mayfield)
Gladys Knight And The Pips in *Claudine* (1974)
ON THE RADIO (Moroder–Summer)
Donna Summer in *Foxes* (1980)
ONE MORE HOUR (Newman)
Jennifer Warnes in *Ragtime* (1981)
ONE TIN SOLDIER (LEGEND OF BILLY JACK) (Lambert–Potter)
Coven in *Billy Jack* (1971)

PASS ME BY (Coleman–Leigh)
Digby Wolfe in *Father Goose* (1965)
(The most popular record version was by Peggy Lee.)
PEOPLE ALONE (Love Theme from *The Competition*) (Schifrin–Jennings)
Randy Crawford in *The Competition* (1980)
PRISONER (Love Theme from EYES OF LAURA MARS) (DeSantels–Lawrence)
Barbra Streisand in *Eyes Of Laura Mars* (1978)

RAINDROPS KEEP FALLIN' ON MY HEAD (Bacharach–David)
B.J. Thomas in *Butch Cassidy And The Sundance Kid* (1969)
REACH FOR THE TOP (Conti–Jenkins–Lerios)
Pablo Cruise in *Dreamer* (1979)
READY TO TAKE THAT CHANCE AGAIN (Fox–Gimbel)
Barry Manilow in *Foul Play* (1978)
RICHARD'S WINDOW (Fox–Gimbel)
Olivia Newton-John in *The Other Side Of The Mountain* (UK: *A Window To The Sky*) (1975)
RUSH, RUSH (Moroder–Harry)
Debbie Harry in *Scarface* (1983)

SEND A LITTLE LOVE MY WAY (Mancini–David)
Anne Murray in *Oklahoma Crude* (1973)

56

THE SHADOW OF YOUR SMILE
(Love Theme from *The Sandpiper*)
(Mandel–Webster)
Studio Chorus in *The Sandpiper*
(1965)
(Tony Bennett had the hit record.)
SO LITTLE TIME (Tiomkin–Webster)
Andy Williams in *55 Days At Peking* (1963)
SOMEBODY'S BABY (Browne–Kortchman)
Jackson Browne in *Fast Times At Ridgemont High* (1982)
SOMEONE WHO CARES (Harvey)
Kenny Rogers in *Fools* (1970)
STAYIN' ALIVE (B., R. and M. Gibb)
The Bee Gees, accompanying the most revered dance sequence since *Singin' In The Rain*, in *Saturday Night Fever* (1977)
(Score also included "Night Fever", "Jive Talkin'" and "How Deep Is Your Love".)

THROUGH THE EYES OF LOVE
(Theme from *Ice Castles*)
(Hamlisch–Sager)

Melissa Manchester in *Ice Castles* (1979)
TILL LOVE TOUCHES YOUR LIFE (Ortolani–Madron)
Richard Williams and Jan Daley in *Madron* (1971)
TOO CLOSE TO PARADISE (Conti–Sager–Roberts)
Sylvester Stallone in *Paradise Alley* (1978)
TWIST OF FATE (Kipner–Beckett)
Olivia Newton-John in *Two Of A Kind* (1983)

UP WHERE WE BELONG (Nitzsche–Jennings–Sainte-Marie)
Joe Cocker and Jennifer Warnes in

Above: The love theme song, "People Alone", from *The Competition* (1980), was sung by Randy Crawford.

Left: The love theme from *The Sandpiper* (1965), sung by the Studio Chorus. Tony Bennett made a hit record of the song.

Fess Parker is best remembered for his portrayals of Davy Crockett and Daniel Boone. In *Westward Ho, The Wagons!* (1956), five new songs were woven into the soundtrack, including "Wringle Wrangle".

An Officer And A Gentleman (1982)
(This was played over the end titles, but is officially referred to as the "Love Theme".)

WHAT ARE YOU DOING THE REST OF YOUR LIFE (Legrand–A. and M. Bergman)
Michael Dees in *The Happy Ending* (1969)
WHAT THE WORLD NEEDS NOW IS LOVE (Bacharach–David)
Jackie De Shannon in *Bob And Carol And Ted And Alice* (1969)
THE WINDMILLS OF YOUR MIND (Legrand–A. and M. Bergman)
Noel Harrison in *The Thomas Crown Affair* (1968)
WITH YOU I'M BORN AGAIN (Shire–Connors)
Billy Preston and Syreeta in *Fastbreak* (1979)

THE WONDERFUL SEASON OF LOVE (Waxman–Webster)
Rosemary Clooney in *Return To Peyton Place* (1961)
WRINGLE WRANGLE (Bruns)
Fess Parker in *Westward Ho, The Wagons!* (1956)
(Rex Allen had the hit record.)

YESTERDAY WHEN I WAS YOUNG (Aznavour–Kretzmer)
Charles Aznavour in *Hustle* (1975)
YOU TAKE MY HEART AWAY (Conti–Connors–Robbins)
DeEtta Little and Nelson Pigford in *Rocky* (1976)
(After "Gonna Fly Now", the other memorable ballad from the first *Rocky* film — a huge UK hit for Little and Pigford, and a US chart entry for James Darren.)

14 "INSPIRED" MOVIE SONGS

The music industry came up with the term "inspired by", not referring to religious-influenced compositions, but to songs specially written either to promote a movie or to take advantage of the media exposure and public response that a particular film is receiving.

Probably the most unusual history of any movie title song belongs to "Alfie" which was never in the original film. Tenor-sax player Sonny Rollins was commissioned to write the music for the British production *Alfie* and, when the film opened in London in 1966, Rollins's jazz score was evident, but with no songs included whatsoever. Burt Bacharach and Hal David subsequently wrote a song called "Alfie" which was successfully recorded by Britain's Cilla Black. Cher was the first to record the song for American audiences, and her version was dubbed onto the soundtrack of the film's North American release, thereby qualifying it to be nominated for the Best Song Oscar at the 1966 Academy Awards.

The Academy's stipulation about a song being audible on the soundtrack had been an issue on previous occasions, particularly in 1954 when the theme "song" from *The High And The Mighty* (Tiomkin–Washington) was initially just whistled on the soundtrack, but Warner Bros. swiftly withdrew the film and added a choral version of the song to ensure its qualification as an Oscar nominee.

Having cited the "Alfie" story, here are six other songs which not only did not appear in the films of which they bear the title, but were not based on any melody heard in the respective scores:

THE MAN WHO SHOT LIBERTY VALANCE (Bacharach–David)
Inspired by 1962's *The Man Who Shot Liberty Valance*.
Recorded by Gene Pitney.

PORTRAIT OF JEANNIE (Robinson–Burdge)
Inspired by 1948's *Portrait Of Jeannie*.
Recorded by Nat "King" Cole.

SINK THE BISMARCK (Horton–Franks)
Probably the most distantly related of all songs to share the title of a motion picture. Recorded in 1960 by the late country singer, Johnny Horton, who built a career singing narrative sagas, single-handedly transformed the British wartime victory into an American Civil War setting!

TO EACH HIS OWN (Livingston Evans)
Inspired by 1946's *To Each His Own*.
Recorded by The Ink Spots, Eddy Howard, Freddy Martin, Tony Martin, and The Modernaires, all of whom had individual best-selling records with the song, as did The Platters, and Frankie Laine when the song was revived in later years. The tune was eventually heard on a soundtrack in 1964, when it was integrated into the score for *The Conversation*.

VERTIGO (Livingston–Evans)

"Wives And Lovers", by Burt Bacharach, was inspired by the 1963 movie of the same name.

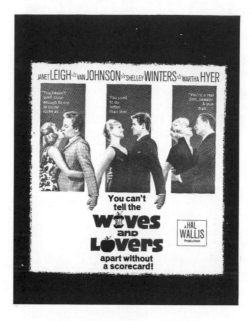

You can't tell the wives and lovers apart without a scorecard!

JANET LEIGH ☆ VAN JOHNSON ☆ SHELLEY WINTERS ☆ MARTHA HYER

A HAL WALLIS Production

Inspired by 1958's *Vertigo*.
Recorded by Billy Eckstine.

WIVES AND LOVERS (Bacharach–David)
Inspired by 1963's *Wives And Lovers*.
Recorded by Jack Jones.

The more regular promotional songs to be born after the film's release are those which are based on existing themes from the soundtracks.

Most such songs are written within a short period of time following the picture's initial appearance; one particular exception, however, was "Smile", written in 1954 by John Turner and Geoffrey Parsons and based on Charles Chaplin's theme from his 1936 film *Modern Times*. (Incidentally, advertisements for this film heralded the comedian singing on-screen for the first time, when the song in question was simply a brief, unintelligible nonsense lyric.)

The following is a selection of the many compositions which were "based on the theme" of major motion pictures.

AROUND THE WORLD (Young–Adamson)
Based on Victor Young's theme from the epic-scale movie *Around The World In 80 Days* (1956), the song became a major hit for Bing Crosby (in both the US and UK), Mantovani (US and UK), The McGuire Sisters (US only), Victor Young (US), Gracie Fields (UK), and Ronnie Hilton (UK). Sadly, Young died before receiving the Oscar for the Best Score of 1956.

CALL OF THE FARAWAY HILLS (Young–David)
Song based on the theme from 1953's western classic *Shane*. Recorded by various artists, including Dolores Gray and Ken Curtis.

EMILY (Mandel–Mercer)
Actually commissioned for use in 1964's *The Americanization Of Emily*, but never finally included. Recorded by Andy Williams.

ETERNALLY (Chaplin–Turner–Parsons)
Vocal version of "Terry's Theme" from Charles Chaplin's 1952 film *Limelight* became a hit for British singer Jimmy Young in 1953.

THE EXODUS SONG (Gold–Boone)
Following the success of "Theme From Exodus" by the piano duo of Ferrante And Teicher, Pat Boone added a lyric and recorded "The Exodus Song" which was subtitled "This Land Is Mine".

FASCINATION (Marcetti–Manning)
The score for 1957's *Love In The Afternoon* included three French

melodies: "C'est Si Bon" (Betti–Hornez), "L'Ame Des Poètes" (Trenet), and this tune, played in the film by a gypsy string quartet. "Fascination" became the hit theme of the picture and, with an English lyric, went on to become a hit record for songstress Jane Morgan.

IT CAN'T BE WRONG (Steiner–Gannon)
The haunting theme from Bette Davis's 1942 classic *Now Voyager* became a successful ballad following the picture's original release when it was recorded by Dick Haymes. More recently, Miss Davis herself recorded the song on an album she made in London in 1973.

LAST TANGO IN PARIS (Barbieri–Previn)
Dory Previn wrote the lyric to Gato Barbieri's main theme from 1972's *Last Tango In Paris*, recorded by Andy Williams, and Marlena Shaw.

LAURA (Raksin–Mercer)
One of the most successful title songs written after a film's release, it was a hit for five separate artists: Woody Herman, Dick Haymes, Freddy Martin, and Johnnie Johnston, all in 1945, with a revival by Stan Kenton in 1951.

LOOK AGAIN (Previn–Langdon)
The 1963 comedy film *Irma La Douce* was based on a Broadway musical but, except for three of the original tunes, the songs were dropped, and after the film came out, Dory (Previn) Langdon lyricised Andre Previn's dominant theme into this ballad, recorded by Adam Wade and Roger Williams.

LOVE FOR LOVE (Korngold–Koehler)
Theme from 1947's *Escape Me Never*, recorded by Claude Thornhill And His Orchestra with Fran Warren.

LOVE LETTERS (Young–Heyman)
Theme from 1945's *Love Letters*,

The score for *Love In The Afternoon* (1957) included three French melodies: "C'est Si Bon", "L'Ame Des Poètes" and "Fascination".

The theme from the classic 1942 movie *Now Voyager* was recorded by its star Bette Davis thirty years later.

"Mam'selle", theme from *The Razor's Edge* (1947), became a hit for Art Lund.

recorded originally by such as Dick Haymes, and revived successfully in later years by both Ketty Lester and Elvis Presley.

MAKE MY DAY (Blackwell)
This memorable song from Clint Eastwood's 1983 movie, *Sudden Impact*, became a country hit for singer T. G. Sheppard, with Eastwood himself providing the necessary dialogue.

MAM'SELLE (Goulding–Gordon)
Theme from the French cafe scene in 1947's *The Razor's Edge*, the song became a hit for Art Lund, and was also recorded by Dick Haymes and Frankie Laine.

MONA LISA (Livingston–Evans)
Though this song is credited as first appearing in 1950's *Captain Carey USA* (UK: *After Midnight*), it was only sung in Italian on the soundtrack. Nat "King" Cole

popularised the English lyric and turned it into a chart-topping hit.

THE MOON OF MANAKOORA (Newman–Loesser)
Alfred Newman's sweeping theme from John Ford's 1937 epic drama, *The Hurricane*, became *Moon Of Manakoora* after the film's release and thence a hit song recorded by the star of that film, Dorothy Lamour.

MY OWN TRUE LOVE (Steiner–David)
The main theme (Tara's) from 1939's classic *Gone With The Wind* gained this lyric in 1941 and was sung by Margaret Whiting.

RACE TO THE END (Vangelis–Anderson)
Based on the hit theme from 1981's *Chariots Of Fire*. First recorded by Jane Olivor, and Melissa Manchester.

SOMETIMES (Davis–Newell)
Written for the 1984 British film, *Champions*, and based on the movie's main theme, this was recorded by Elaine Paige specially for the soundtrack, but was removed before the picture was released.

SOMEWHERE MY LOVE (Jarre–Webster)
The majestic theme from 1965's *Doctor Zhivago* became the much-sung "Somewhere My Love", recorded primarily by The Ray Conniff Singers.

SPEAK SOFTLY LOVE (Rota–Kusik)
The love theme from 1971's *The Godfather* was recorded under this title by both Andy Williams and one of the stars of the film

itself, Al Martino.

STELLA BY STARLIGHT (Young–Washington)

Theme from 1944's ghost story *The Uninvited*. Victor Young released it orchestrally and the song was also cut by Nat "King" Cole, and The Three Suns.

STRANGERS IN THE NIGHT (Kaempfert–Snyder–Singleton)

Frank Sinatra had a major success with this song, based on a melody from Bert Kaempfert's score for 1966's *A Man Could Get Killed*.

THE SUMMER KNOWS (Legrand–A. and M. Bergman)

Based on the theme from 1971's *Summer Of '42*, this ballad recorded by Andy Williams, among many other artists, is one of the fine collaborations between Michel Legrand and lyricists Alan and Marilyn Bergman.

THEME FROM A SUMMER PLACE (Steiner–Discant)

Originally this theme was an orchestral hit for Percy Faith when the 1959 film *A Summer Place* was released. The lyric, added later, gave The Lettermen a major bestseller in 1965.

THIS IS MY SONG (Chaplin)

The vocal version of Charles Chaplin's theme from his 1965 movie *A Countess From Hong Kong* (apparently contested by French composer Charles Trenet as identical to the opening bars of his 1941 song "Romance Of Paris") provided major hit records for Petula Clark and Harry Secombe.

A TIME FOR US (Rota–Kusik–Snyder)

Song based on the main theme from 1969's *Romeo And Juliet*. A vocal version of the same theme appears on the original soundtrack as "What Is Youth" (Rota–Walter) sung by Glenn Weston. When Henry Mancini successfully recorded the "Love Theme", he featured an orchestral arrangement with chorus included, but without either lyric. Johnny Mathis had the best-selling version of "A Time For Us".

TO BE OR NOT TO BE (THE HITLER RAP) (Brooks–Wingfield)

With this 1984 single, which became a major British hit, Mel Brooks appeared to be setting a new trend for himself: recording concept singles based on, but not featured in, his own comedies.

WHEN I FALL IN LOVE (Young–Heyman)

Though stars Robert Mitchum and Ann Blyth briefly sang "Tell Me, Golden Moon" (Bennett) in 1952's *One Minute To Zero*, the film's main theme didn't become a song until later. Nat "King" Cole was one of the first to record the lyric.

WHERE DO I BEGIN (Lai–Sigman)

Actually copyrighted as "Where Do I Begin (Love Story)", the haunting theme from 1970's *Love Story* became a much recorded item as an instrumental as well as a song, and again, Andy Williams led the field in vocal performances.

15 TELEVISION THEME SONGS

Here is a checklist covering some of the most popular television signature tunes. While the majority are theme songs, certain key instrumental melodies are included, along with the relevant names of hit recording artists where they differ from the original soundtrack performers.

AND THEN THERE'S MAUDE
  Donny Hathaway in *Maude* (1972)
AS TIME GOES BY (Hupfeld)
  Scatman Crothers in *Casablanca* (1983)

THE BALLAD OF DAVY CROCKETT (Blackburn–Bruns)
  Fess Parker in the Davy Crockett episodes of *Disneyland* (1954)
THE BALLAD OF JED CLAMPETT (Flatt–Scruggs)
  Lester Flatt and Earl Scruggs in *The Beverly Hillbillies* (1962)
THE BALLAD OF PALADIN (Boone–Western–Rolfe)
  Johnny Western in *Have Gun, Will Travel* (1957)
  (Recorded successfully by Duane Eddy.)
BATMAN (Hefti)
  Neal Hefti's Orchestra And Chorus in *Batman* (1966)
  (Recorded successfully by Neal Hefti, The Marketts, and Jan And Dean. Same theme also used in the subsequent 1966 movie spin-off.)
BELIEVE IT OR NOT (Post–Geyer)
  Joey Scarbury in *The Greatest American Hero* (1981)

BLUE STAR (THE MEDIC THEME) (Young–Heyman)
  Song based on the theme from (but not heard in) the series *Medic* (1954)
  (Felicia Sanders had the hit record.)
BONANZA (Livingston–Evans)
  Bonanza (1959)
  (Al Caiola had the instrumental hit version; the best-selling vocal record was by Johnny Cash.)

BRIAN'S SONG (Legrand)
  in *Brian's Song* (1972)
  (Michel Legrand charted with this, the first hit theme from an American-produced television movie.)

CHICO AND THE MAN (Feliciano)
  Jose Feliciano in *Chico And The Man* (1974)

DIFFERENT WORLDS (Fox–Gimbel)
  Maureen McGovern in *Angie* (1979)
DISCO LUCY (Daniele–Adamson)
  Disco version of the theme from *I Love Lucy* (1951)
  Recorded in 1977 by The Wilton Place Street Band.
DRAGNET (Schumann)
  Studio Orchestra in *Dragnet* (1951)
  (Ray Anthony had a hit record with the theme in 1953, and comedian Stan Freberg parodied both the melody and the show in a hit single called "St. George And The Dragonet".)

Theme from THE DUKES OF HAZZARD (GOOD OL' BOYS) (Jennings)
Waylon Jennings in *The Dukes Of Hazzard* (1979)

FAME (Gore–Pitchford)
The Kids From Fame in *Fame* (1981)
(Series spun off the 1980 movie retained the hit song.)

FRIENDS FOREVER (Goldenberg–Connors)
Tony Randall, Swoosie Kurtz and Kaleena Kiff in *Love, Sidney* (1981).
Sung over closing credits of the second series by Gladys Knight and Bubba Knight.

GREEN ACRES (Mizzy)
Eddie Albert and Eva Gabor in *Green Acres* (1965)

HAPPY DAYS (Fox–Gimbel)
Studio Chorus in *Happy Days* (from 1976)
(Truett Pratt and Jerry McLain had the hit record. The show, which began in 1974, was originally opened by Bill Haley singing "Rock Around The Clock".)

HARPER VALLEY PTA (Hall)
Uncredited singer in *Harper Valley* (1981)
(The 1968 Jeannie C. Riley record inspired a 1979 movie which, when first screened successfully on network television, gave birth to a small screen sitcom version.)

HAWAII FIVE-O (Stevens)
Studio Orchestra conducted by Morton Stevens in *Hawaii Five-O* (1968)
(The Ventures had the hit version.)

HILL STREET BLUES (Post)

Mike Post with Larry Carlton in *Hill Street Blues* (1980)

HOW SOON (Mancini–Stillman)
Studio Orchestra in *The Richard Boone Show* (1963)
(Henry Mancini, with his Orchestra and Chorus, had a major British hit with this theme in 1964.)

I'M JUST WILD ABOUT HARRY (Sissle–Blake)
Al Jolson in *Goodtime Harry* (1980)
(An original recording of Jolson

Eddie Albert and Eva Gabor sang the title song of their *Green Acres* comedy series (1965).

Edd Byrnes shows off the sheet music of his 1959 hit song, "Kookie, Kookie, Lend Me Your Comb", which was featured during an episode of 77 Sunset Strip (1958).

was used on the soundtrack of this short-lived series.)

KEEP YOUR EYE ON THE SPARROW (BARETTA'S THEME)
Sammy Davis Jr. in Baretta (1975)
(Rhythm Heritage had the hit record.)

KOOKIE, KOOKIE, LEND ME YOUR COMB (Taylor)
Novelty song featured by Edd Byrnes and Connie Stevens during an episode of 77 Sunset Strip
(Edd Byrnes was resident on the show which began in 1958, while Connie Stevens starred in a parallel Warner Bros. series, Hawaiian Eye.)
(Many television stars attempted

to extend their popularity by cutting pop records, including Robert Horton of Wagon Train, Lorne Greene and Michael Landon of Bonanza, Vince Edwards of Ben Casey, Hugh O'Brian of Wyatt Earp, Ted Cassidy of The Addams Family and even David McCallum of The Man From UNCLE. The most successful were Walter Brennan of The Real McCoys, Patty Duke of The Patty Duke Show, Shelley Fabares of The Donna Reed Show, Ricky Nelson from The Adventures Of Ozzie And Harriet and, much later, David Soul of Starsky And Hutch, plus those noted in the "Singing Actors" section following this listing.)

THE LONE RANGER
All the original half-hour Lone Ranger shows opened and closed with an adaptation of Rossini's "William Tell Overture", which had already become the Ranger's signature tune on radio. It also appeared in John Barry's score for The Legend Of The Lone Ranger movie in 1980.
For the latter, Merle Haggard sang a new song titled "Man With The Mask" (Haggard–Pitchford). However, there was an earlier song called "Hi-Yo Silver" (Baxter–Adelson), first heard in the 1958 theatrical feature The Lone Ranger And The Lost City Of Gold. The same song is also used over the credits of some feature-length groupings of episodes from the colour television series.

MAKIN' IT (Perren–Fekaris)
David Naughton in Makin' It (1979)

MAKING OUR DREAMS COME TRUE (Fox–Gimbel)
Cyndi Grecco in *Laverne And Shirley* (1976)

Song from M*A*S*H (SUICIDE IS PAINLESS) (Mandel–Altman)
Studio Orchestra in *M*A*S*H* (1972)
(Johnny Mandel's theme from the original 1970 movie was retained for the television series; its biggest record success was by a studio group called The Mash, arranged and conducted by Mandel himself, and the single topped the British charts in the spring of 1980.)

Theme from THE MONKEES (HEY, HEY, WE'RE THE MONKEES) (Boyce–Hart)
The Monkees (Davy Jones, Peter Tork, Michael Nesmith and Mickey Dolenz) in *The Monkees* (1966)

MR LUCKY (Mancini)
Studio Orchestra in *Mr Lucky* (1960)
(Henry Mancini himself had the hit record.)

(WAIT 'TIL YOU SEE) MY GIDGET (Greenfield–Keller)
Johnny Tillotson in *Gidget* (1965)
(Tillotson was a major pop record seller in the early 1960s, and Greenfield–Keller were a hot writing team, having given Connie Francis two of her biggest hits.)

NADIA'S THEME (DeVorzon–Botkin)
Studio Orchestra in *The Young And The Restless* (1976)
(Barry DeVorzon and Perry Botkin Jr. recorded and took their own theme into the Top Ten record charts, making it the most successful signature tune ever from an American daytime soap opera.)

NINE TO FIVE (Parton)
Stevie Snow (in initial four shows only), and Dolly Parton, who re-recorded the song and whose version is heard in all the later shows, in *9 To 5* (1982)

NO OTHER LOVE (Rodgers–Hammerstein)
Theme from one segment of the 1952 documentary series *Victory At Sea*.
("No Other Love" became a 1953 hit song for Perry Como.)

THE PINK PANTHER THEME (Mancini)
Studio Orchestra in *The Pink Panther* cartoon series (1969)
(Theme originally written for the first *Pink Panther* movie in 1964, and subsequently featured in all the Mirsch Panther cartoons, both theatrical and on television.)

RAWHIDE (Tiomkin–Washington)
Frankie Laine in *Rawhide* (1959)

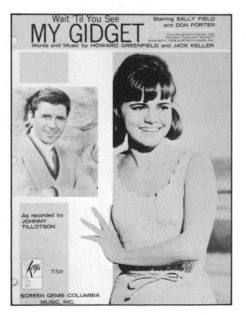

Before Sally Field appeared in the television series *The Flying Nun*, she starred in the series *Gidget*, a spin-off from the 1959 movie success.

Theme song from the television production of *77 Sunset Strip* (1958).

77 SUNSET STRIP

Words and Music by
MACK DAVID and JERRY LIVINGSTON

From the Warner Bros.
TV Show "77 Sunset Strip"

M. WITMARK & SONS
NEW YORK, N. Y.

PRICE 50¢ U.S.A.

(Besides his movie title songs, Frankie Laine had also sung the theme song "Champion, The Wonder Horse" in the 1955 western series, *The Adventures Of Champion*. "Rawhide" was also recorded by one of the show's stars, Sheb Wooley, on his "Songs From The Days Of Rawhide" album. Wooley, himself a gold-disc winner for his 1958 novelty hit "The Purple People Eater", also recorded comedy spoofs under the name "Ben Colder".)

THE ROCKFORD FILES (Post)
Studio Orchestra in *The Rockford Files* (1975)

Theme from ROOTS (Fried)
The 1977 award-winning mini-series contained music composed by Gerald Fried and Quincy Jones. Jones himself charted with a "Roots" medley containing the main theme.

ROUTE 66 (Riddle)
Studio Orchestra in *Route 66* (1960)
(Nelson Riddle himself had the hit record.)

SECRET AGENT MAN (Sloan–Barri)
Johnny Rivers in *Secret Agent* (1965)

77 SUNSET STRIP (David–Livingston)
Studio Chorus in *77 Sunset Strip* (1958)
(Don Ralke had the most successful commercial recording.)

STACCATO'S THEME (Bernstein)
Studio Orchestra in *Johnny Staccato* (also known as *Staccato*) (1959)
(Elmer Bernstein had a Top Ten British hit with this theme.)

THAT WAS THE WEEK THAT WAS (Brahms–Sherrin–Grainer)
The title song (with topical lyric) from David Frost's 1964 series, sung by Millicent Martin (in England), and by Nancy Ames in the American version of the same format.

THERE'S A NEW GIRL IN TOWN (Shire–A. and M. Bergman)
Linda Lavin in *Alice* (1976)

THOSE WERE THE DAYS (Strouse–Adams)
Carroll O'Connor and Jean Stapleton in the 1978–79 season of *All In The Family*. Instrumentally, the same theme introduced later episodes and was later used over the titles of the spin-off, *Archie Bunker's Place*.

THREE STARS WILL SHINE TO-NIGHT (Goldsmith–Rugolo–Winn)
Song based on the theme from *Dr Kildare* (1961 series) and re-

corded successfully by the show's star, Richard Chamberlain.

THE TRAVELS OF JAMIE Mc-PHEETERS
The Osmond Brothers in *The Travels Of Jamie McPheeters* (1963)
(The Osmond Brothers (later The Osmonds) were heard on the soundtrack of each show, and themselves appeared in certain episodes. The series featured 16-year-old Kurt Russell, who starred in the vidpic *Elvis* in 1979.)

WELCOME BACK (Sebastian)
John Sebastian in *Welcome Back, Kotter* (1975)
WHERE EVERYBODY KNOWS YOUR NAME (Theme from *Cheers*) (Portnoy–Angelo)
Gary Portnoy in *Cheers* (1973)

YOU LOOK AT ME (Phillips–Dunne)
Scott Baio and Erin Moran in *Joanie Loves Chachi* (1981)

ZORRO (Bruns–Foster)
Henry Calvin in *Zorro* (1957)
(The Chordettes had the hit record.)

Television movies have also contributed some memorable music scores, including Henry Mancini's poignant title theme from 1971's *Brian's Song*, and the Stephen Lawrence–Bruce Hart compositions for 1979's *Sooner Or Later*, sung on the soundtrack by Rex Smith, and including the chartmaking title song. From a 1955 television production of *Our Town* came Frank Sinatra's hit "Love And Marriage" (Van Heusen–Cahn). Like Mancini, composer John Barry has written some distinguished television themes, including "Hit And Miss" (the signature tune

THEME FROM "DR. KILDARE"
(THREE STARS WILL SHINE TONIGHT)
Lyric by HAL WINN
Music by JERRALD GOLDSMITH · PETE RUGOLO
An MGM-TV Production in association with NBC-TV
MATCH-A-CHORD FOR ALL ORGANS
Recorded by RICHARD CHAMBERLAIN on M-G-M RECORDS
WHEN PERFORMING THIS COMPOSITION PLEASE GIVE ALL PROGRAM CREDITS TO
HASTINGS MUSIC CORPORATION
1540 Broadway · New York 36, N.Y.
PRICE 60¢ IN U.S.A.

"Three Stars Will Shine Tonight", the theme song from *Dr Kildare* (1961 series), was recorded successfully by the show's star, Richard Chamberlain.

of BBC Television's British version of *Juke Box Jury*, recorded in 1960 by his rock group, The John Barry Seven), *The Persuaders* in 1971, the 1973 series of *Orson Welles Great Mysteries*, plus the score to 1978's television movie remake of *The Corn Is Green*. It was also John Barry who wrote the music for the 1963 television special *Elizabeth Taylor In London*, one of a number of programmes over the years to have been built around non-musical movie stars. In 1967, Gilbert Becaud and Rod McKuen wrote "The Importance Of The Rose" for a Grace Kelly television special, *Monte Carlo, C'est La Rose*.

16 THE SINGING ACTORS

Reportedly, numerous careers perished when sound movies replaced the silent era, with audiences unable to adjust to the voices of certain recognisable faces. Aside from musical performers, actors-turned-singers are an interesting breed, and a number of recording artists have emerged from the ranks of the usually non-singing actors.

A good case in point is Robert Mitchum, who has sung periodically in his own pictures. He also co-wrote "The Ballad Of Thunder Road" (Raye–Mitchum) for the 1958 movie, and sang it into popularity; almost a decade later he returned to the same charts with his recording of "Little Ol' Wine Drinker Me" (Mills–Jennings). Jeff Chandler sang and co-wrote (with Henry Mancini) the title song in 1955's *Foxfire*, as well as cutting some commercial discs.

Both Messrs Mitchum and Chandler were no strangers to western films, and the Hollywood singing cowboys, including Gene Autry, Roy Rogers, Tex Ritter, Jimmy Wakeley, Eddie Dean, and Smiley Burnette, also pursued recording careers concurrent with their movie-making.

In fact, the list of Hollywood actors who have recorded commercially over the years is seemingly endless, including Tony Perkins, Charles Boyer, Anthony Quinn, Maureen O'Hara, Rhonda Fleming, Telly Savalas, Jack Carson, Eddie Albert, Lizabeth Scott, Bette Davis, Vincent Price, George Chakiris, Jose Ferrer, Tony Randall, Larry Hagman, John Wayne, George Maharis, Dale Robertson, George Sanders, Constance Towers, Richard Chamberlain, and even Robert Wagner, who was being groomed as a record teen-idol in 1957, presumably following the chart-topper that year by fellow-actor Tab Hunter, titled "Young Love" (Joyner–Cartey).

Today, the trend continues with such as Clint Eastwood, Mel Brooks, and Burt Reynolds available at your local record store, along with such television performers as Rick Springfield, John Schneider, and The Kids From Fame.

SINGING ABOUT ACTORS

One by-product of the superstar syndrome is the tribute song, and probably the best example of a lyric referring to a major star is "Dear Mr Gable", the introductory verse written by Roger Edens specially for Judy Garland; it was used in 1937's *Broadway Melody Of 1938*, with 15-year-old Judy writing a fan letter as she gazes at a framed portrait of Clark Gable.

Following the death in 1926 of silent screen idol, Rudolph Valentino, "There's A New Star In Heaven Tonight" (McHugh–Mills–Brennan) became a hit of the day and it was revived by Richard Day-Lewis on the soundtrack of the 1978 biopic *Valentino*. There was even a novelty song in the '40s called "The Humphrey Bogart Rhumba", while other star tributes have included "Candle In The Wind" (Elton John and Bernie Taupin's homage to Marilyn Monroe), Neil Sedaka's opus to "Betty Grable", the Kim Carnes best-seller "Bette Davis Eyes" (DeShannon–Weiss), and, from 1944, "Nancy (With The Laughing

ED 2160

JEFF CHANDLER SINGS

DECCA RECORDS EXTENDED PLAY 45

I SHOULD CARE
MORE THAN ANYONE
LAMPLIGHT
THAT'S ALL SHE'S WAITING TO HEAR

A commercial disc cut by Hollywood actor Jeff Chandler. He also sang and co-wrote, with Henry Mancini, the title song of *Foxfire* (1955).

Face)" written by composer James Van Heusen and comedian Phil Silvers for Frank Sinatra, and dedicated to Frank's daughter who has since become a recording star in her own right.

Among the most recent songs about actors are: "Bogart", written and recorded by Nik Kershaw; "The Curly Shuffle" (Quinn), recorded by Jump 'N The Saddle, and dedicated to Curly of the Three Stooges; "Dear Michael" (Willenski–Davis), recorded by Kim Fields (star of television's *The Facts of Life*), a contemporary version of the "Dear Mr Gable" concept addressed to Michael Jackson; "Key Largo" (Higgins–Limbo), referring to Bogart and Bacall, recorded by Bertie Higgins; "Marie Provost", about the silent movie actress, written and recorded by Nick Lowe; "Michael Caine" (Smyth–Woodgate), recorded by Madness; and "Robert De Niro's Waiting" (Jolley–Swain–Dallin–Fahey–Woodward), recorded by Bananarama.

17 THE SINGERS AND THE SONGS IN NON-MUSICALS

Before discussing movie musical songs, it seems only fair to examine a few of those hundreds of songs featured in dramatic pictures.

So often, key numbers are performed in such settings as bar-rooms and nightclubs, or they are included as brief asides by the leading man or woman. This use of music has always intrigued me, and all too rarely have such examples been documented.

Whether it's Angela Lansbury as the music-hall singer in 1945's *The Picture Of Dorian Gray*, timidly giving forth "Goodbye Little Yellow Bird" (Hargreaves–O'Brien), or dear old Harry Davenport launching into a chorus of "A-Tisket, A-Tasket" (Feldman–Fitzgerald) in 1938's *The Cowboy And The Lady*, or pianist George Segal and drummer Glenda Jackson singing "She Loves Me, She Told Me So Last Night" (Frank) in 1973's *A Touch Of Class*, or even Yul Brynner, decked out in drag as a female singer performing Noel Coward's "Mad About The Boy" to an attentive Roman Polanski in 1970's *The Magic Christian*, they all merit being credited, and so the following brief list gives a few such moments deserved recognition.

Also included are a sampling of those professional singers who appear fronting bands or small groups whenever a song is required, as in the cases of Larry Burke singing "Believe Me If All Those Endearing Young Charms" (Moore) in the nightclub sequence from the 1945 film *Those Endearing Young Charms*, in which Ann Harding as Laraine Day's mother realises that the song brings back tearful memories; and composer–pianist Matt Dennis playing and singing, "It Wasn't The Stars That Thrilled Me" (Dennis–Gilliam) as Edmond O'Brien dances with Ida Lupino in 1953's *The Bigamist*.

The section "Who Sang What For Whom" explains how certain actors are dubbed by off-screen singers. A few of these cases are indicated in the following entries, but it should be noted that certain other performers listed may not have used their own voices even though I have not indicated substitutes.

AFTER YOU'VE GONE (Creamer–Layton)
    Marsha Hunt in a party scene in *Unholy Partners* (1941)
    Shirley MacLaine in *Some Came Running* (1958)
AGAIN (Newman–Cochran)
    Ida Lupino, as the singer hired by Richard Widmark, in *Road House* (1948)
    Warren Stevens, briefly in a club scene, in *Phone Call From A Stranger* (1952)
ALL BY MYSELF (Schwartz–Dietz)
    Jerry Lewis in *The Delicate Delinquent* (1957)
ALL I DO IS DREAM OF YOU (Brown–Freed)
    Gene Raymond in *Sadie McKee* (1934)
ALL THROUGH THE NIGHT (Schwartz–Mercer)
    Kaaren Verne in a club scene in *All Through The Night* (1942)

Ida Lupino introduces "Again" in *Road House* (1948).

Andy Williams gives little attention to the road as he serenades Sandra Dee in *I'd Rather Be Rich* (1964).

ALMOST THERE (Shayne–Keller)
Andy Williams to Sandra Dee in *I'd Rather Be Rich* (1964)

This song was featured in the most famous of the Marx Brothers' films, *A Night At The Opera* (1935).

Joan Crawford, who could also sing and dance, gave a rendition of "Always And Always" in *Mannequin* (1937).

ALONE (Brown–Freed)
Allan Jones and Kitty Carlisle in *A Night At The Opera* (1935)
Judy Garland in *Andy Hardy Meets A Debutante* (1940)

ALWAYS (Berlin)
Betty Avery with Ray Noble And His Orchestra in *Pride Of The Yankees* (1942)
Deanna Durbin in *Christmas Holiday* (1944)

ALWAYS AND ALWAYS (Ward–Forrest–Wright)
Joan Crawford, dancing with Alan Curtis, in *Mannequin* (1937)

AM I BLUE (Akst–Clarke)
Hoagy Carmichael and Lauren Bacall in *To Have And Have Not* (1944)

AND HER TEARS FLOWED LIKE WINE (Kenton–Lawrence–Greene)
Lauren Bacall in *The Big Sleep* (1946)

AND THE MOON GREW BRIGHTER AND BRIGHTER (Kennedy–Singer)
Kirk Douglas, accompanying himself on banjo, in *Man Without A Star* (1955)

AND THERE YOU ARE (Fain–Koehler)
Van Johnson with Xavier Cugat And His Orchestra in *Weekend At The Waldorf* (1945)

AQUI (Newman–Darby)
Rita Moreno as the cafe singer in a Mexican port in *Garden Of Evil* (1954)

AS TIME GOES BY (Hupfeld)
Dooley Wilson, as the singer in Rick's Cafe, to both Humphrey Bogart and Ingrid Bergman (the latter also humming the opening phrase), in *Casablanca* (1942)
(Dooley Wilson's performance of the song was included in original

Lauren Bacall takes over the song of "Am I Blue" from Hoagy Carmichael in *To Have And Have Not* (1944).

Casablanca footage used in Woody Allen's 1972 film *Play It Again, Sam*.)
Barbra Streisand to Ryan O'Neal in *What's Up Doc* (1972)
AT THE BALL, THAT'S ALL (Hill)
The Avalon Boys (including Chill Wills), providing accompaniment for Stan Laurel and Oliver Hardy's famous two-step dance routine, in *Way Out West* (1937)
ATLANTIC CITY, MY OLD FRIEND (Anka)
Ann Burns, Marie Burns and Jean Burns in *Atlantic City* (1981)

Humphrey Bogart and Ingrid Bergman look on as Dooley Wilson sits at the piano in *Casablanca* (1942). The hit record came 35 years after the film's original release.

Frances Farmer sings with Walter Brennan and Edward Arnold in *Come And Get It* (1936). Her featured song, "Aura Lee", is the Union Army song which was later adapted as "Love Me Tender".

AURA LEE (Fosdick–Poulton)
Frances Farmer in *Come And Get It* (1936)

BABY, THE RAIN MUST FALL (Bernstein–Sheldon)
Billy Strange for Steve McQueen in *Baby The Rain Must Fall* (1964)
(Glen Campbell plays a member of Steve McQueen's back-up band.)

(THE BOYS ARE) BACK IN TOWN (O'Neal)
The Busboys in *48 Hrs* (1982)

THE BAD IN EVERY MAN (the original version of "Blue Moon") (Rodgers–Hart)
Shirley Ross in *Manhattan Melodrama* (1934)

THE BALLAD OF CAT BALLOU (Livingston–David)
Nat "King" Cole and Stubby Kaye in *Cat Ballou* (1965)

BALLIN' THE JACK (Smith–Burris)
Dean Martin in *That's My Boy* (1951)

BECAUSE OF YOU (Wilkinson–Hammerstein)
Ann Dvorak in *I Was An American Spy* (1951)
(In 1952 a romantic drama titled *Because Of You*, starring Loretta Young and Jeff Chandler, used the original melody throughout.)

BEI MIR BIST DU SCHON (Means That You're Grand) (Secunda–Jacobs–Chaplin–Cahn)
Priscilla Lane in *Love, Honor And Obey* (1938)

THE BELLS OF ST. MARY'S (Burke–Van Heusen)
Bing Crosby with The Robert Mitchell Boychoir in *The Bells Of St. Mary's* (1945)

BEST FRIEND (Reddy–Burton)
Helen Reddy in *Airport 1975* (1975)

BETTER THAN EVER (Hamlisch–

In *Baby The Rain Must Fall*, Steve McQueen is restrained by his musicians, including an uncredited Glen Campbell.

Sager)

Candice Bergen in *Starting Over* (1979)

(Also sung by Stephanie Mills over final credits.)

BIG ROCK CANDY MOUNTAIN (Traditional)

William Holden and a children's chorus in *Father Is A Bachelor* (1950)

BING! BANG! BONG! (Livingston–Evans)

Sophia Loren with a children's chorus in *Houseboat* (1958)

A BIRD IN A GILDED CAGE (Tilzer–Lamb)

Joan Crawford and Fred Mac-

Murray in *Above Suspicion* (1943)

BLACK MARKET (Hollander)

Marlene Dietrich as the cabaret singer in a basement club in *A Foreign Affair* (1948)

BLOW THAT HORN (Wright–Forrest–Donaldson)

Dorothy McNulty (later known as Penny Singleton) in *After The Thin Man* (1936)

THE BLUE GARDENIA (Russell–Lee)

Nat "King" Cole in *The Blue Gardenia* (1953)

BLUE MOON (Rodgers–Hart)

Valentina Cortesa in *Malaya* (1949)

(See also "The Bad In Every Man".)

77

The Bob Hope–Jane Russell comedy *The Paleface* featured the hit "Buttons And Bows".

BLUES IN THE NIGHT (Arlen–Mercer)
Unbilled singer and Jimmy Lunceford And His Orchestra in *Blues In The Night* (1941)
John Garfield, parodying his gangster image, in *Thank Your Lucky Stars* (1943)

BODY AND SOUL (Green–Heyman–Sour–Eyton)
Janis Paige in *Her Kind Of Man* (1946)
Peg LaCentra for Ida Lupino in *The Man I Love* (1947)

BOOGIE WOOGIE BUGLE BOY FROM COMPANY B (Raye–Prince)
The Andrews Sisters in *Buck Privates* (1941)

THE BOYS IN THE BACKROOM (Hollander–Loesser)
Marlene Dietrich, singing in The Last Chance saloon, in *Destry Rides Again* (1939)

THE BRAMBLE BUSH (DeVol–David)

Trini Lopez in *The Dirty Dozen* (1967)

BUTTONS AND BOWS (Livingston–Evans)
Bob Hope and Jane Russell, as well as Roy Rogers, in *The Paleface* (1948)

BYE BYE BLACKBIRD (Henderson–Dixon)
Jason Robards as Howard Hughes in *Melvin And Howard* (1980)

CALL ME IRRESPONSIBLE (Van Heusen–Cahn)
Jackie Gleason in *Papa's Delicate Condition* (1963)

A CERTAIN SMILE (Fain–Webster)
Johnny Mathis in *A Certain Smile* (1958)

THE CHILDREN'S MARCHING SONG (THIS OLD MAN) (traditional arranged by Arnold)
Ingrid Bergman and a children's chorus in *Inn Of The Sixth Happiness* (1958)

CITY OF THE ONE-NIGHT STANDS (Baskin)
Richard Baskin and Keith Carradine in *Welcome To LA* (1976)

COCKTAILS FOR TWO (Coslow–Johnston)
Spike Jones And His City Slickers in *Ladies' Man* (1947)
(First sung by Carl Brisson in 1934's *Murder At The Vanities*.)

COOL WATER (Nolan)
Roy Rogers in *Along The Navajo Trail* (1945)

DID I REMEMBER (Adamson–Donaldson)
Jean Harlow, the showgirl, and Cary Grant, the flyer, in *Suzy* (1936)

DON'T BLAME ME (McHugh–Fields)
Betty Garrett in *Big City* (1948)
Peggy King, at a Hollywood

party, in *The Bad And The Beautiful* (1952)

Leslie Uggams in *Two Weeks In Another Town* (1962)

DON'T CRY LITTLE FISH (Waxman–Kahn)

Spencer Tracy, accompanying himself on a hurdy-gurdy, in *Captains Courageous* (1937)

DOO WAH DIDDY-DIDDY (Greenwich–Barry)

Bill Murray and Harold Ramis, leading their platoon, in *Stripes* (1981)

DREAM LOVER (Schertzinger–Grey)

Claudette Colbert, to Ray Milland as they dance, in *Arise My Love* (1940)

(First sung by Jeanette MacDonald in 1929's *The Love Parade*; later included in the score of 1944's *Lady In The Dark*.)

Virginia Verrill sang for Jean Harlow "Did I Remember" in *Suzy* (1936).

DRUM BOOGIE (Krupa-Eldridge)

Barbara Stanwyck with Gene Krupa And His Orchestra in *Ball Of Fire* (1942)

(Krupa's own original recording of "Drum Boogie" heard on the soundtrack of *Raging Bull* in 1980.)

DRY BONES (Traditional)

Peter O'Toole, leading the hunt, in *The Ruling Class* (1971)

EE-O ELEVEN (Van Heusen–Cahn)

Sammy Davis Jr. in *Ocean's 11* (1960)

EITHER IT'S LOVE OR IT ISN'T (Roberts–Fisher)

Lizabeth Scott, as the night-club singer ("Cinderella with the husky voice"), to Humphrey Bogart, in *Dead Reckoning* (1947)

EVERYBODY LOVES MY BABY (BUT MY BABY DON'T LOVE NOBODY BUT ME) (Williams–Palmer)

Rosalind Russell, joined briefly by Sandra Dee, in *Rosie!* (1967)

EV'RYONE SAYS 'I LOVE YOU' (Ruby–Kalmar)

Groucho, Chico, Zeppo, and played by Harpo, all on individual occasions, in *Horse Feathers* (1932)

FALLING IN LOVE AGAIN (Hollander–Lerner)

Marlene Dietrich, as Lola-Lola of the Blue Angel cafe, in *The Blue Angel* (1930)

FAREWELL AMANDA (Porter)

David Wayne, to Katharine Hepburn as Amanda Bonner, in *Adam's Rib* (1949)

(The song briefly reprised in the same film by means of a phonograph record featuring Frank Sinatra's voice.)

FINICULI, FINICULA (Denza)

William Holden, Lee J. Cobb, Sam Levene, William Strauss, and

Beatrice Blinn at the piano in *Golden Boy* (1939)

THE FIRST TIME I SAW YOU (Shilkret–Wrubel)
Frances Farmer in *The Toast Of New York* (1937)
(A year later, Joe Penner — as a singing bank teller — sang the opening bars in *Go Chase Yourself*.)
(The song subsequently became the recurring theme in the 1947 film noir classic, *Out Of The Past*, released in the UK as *Build My Gallows High*.)

GETTING TO KNOW YOU (Rodgers–Hammerstein)
Henry Winkler in *The One And Only* (1978)

GLORY ALLEY (Livingston–David)
Louis Armstrong to Ralph Meeker and others in a New Orleans club in *Glory Alley* (1952)

THE GLORY OF LOVE (Hill)
Jacqueline Fontaine, the cabaret singer, in *Guess Who's Coming To Dinner* (1967)
(This song, dating back to the '30s, was featured throughout *Guess Who's Coming To Dinner*, and sung over the opening titles by a chorus.)

GOLDEN EARRINGS (Young–Livingston–Evans)
Marlene Dietrich and Murvyn Vye as gypsies in *Golden Earrings* (1947)

GOODNIGHT SWEETHEART Noble – Campbell – Connelly – Vallee)
Rudy Vallee, serenading Claudette Colbert beneath her bedroom window, in *The Palm Beach Story* (1942)

HIGH ANXIETY (Brooks)

Mel Brooks, parodying cabaret performers, in *High Anxiety* (1977)

HIGH HOPES (Van Heusen–Cahn)
Frank Sinatra with Eddie Hodges in *A Hole In The Head* (1959)

HOLD YOUR MAN (Brown–Freed)
Jean Harlow speaks the lyric to piano accompaniment in *Hold Your Man* (1933)

HOME COOKIN' (Livingston–Evans)
Bob Hope and Lucille Ball in *Fancy Pants* (1950)

HOME ON THE RANGE (Traditional)
James Burke, the cop, at the request of Henry Fonda, in *The Mad Miss Manton* (1938)
Cary Grant, in the shower, in *Mr Blandings Builds His Dream House* (1948)
The Sons Of The Pioneers in *Fighting Coast Guard* (1951)

HONG KONG BLUES (Carmichael)
Hoagy Carmichael in *To Have And Have Not* (1944)

HOT VOODOO (Coslow–Rainger)
Marlene Dietrich, in a gorilla suit, in *Blonde Venus* (1932)

THE HOUSE I LIVE IN (THAT'S AMERICA TO ME) (Robinson–Allan) Frank Sinatra in *The House I Live In* (1945 short subject)

HOW ABOUT YOU (Lane–Freed)
Anne Bancroft, the bar-room singer, in *Don't Bother To Knock* (1952)

HOW LITTLE WE KNOW (Carmichael–Mercer)
Hoagy Carmichael and Lauren Bacall in *To Have And Have Not* (1944)

I CAN'T BELIEVE THAT YOU'RE IN LOVE WITH ME (McHugh–Gaskill)
Claudia Drake, as Tom Neal's girlfriend, in *Detour* (1946)
May Wynn, as Robert Francis's

girl, in *The Caine Mutiny* (1954)

I CAN'T GIVE YOU ANYTHING BUT LOVE, BABY (McHugh–Fields)
Cary Grant and Katharine Hepburn, pursuing an escaped leopard, in *Bringing Up Baby* (1938)
Marlene Dietrich in *Seven Sinners* (1940)

I COULDN'T SLEEP A WINK LAST NIGHT (Adamson–McHugh)
Martha O'Driscoll in *Criminal Court* (1946)

I DARE YOU (Freed–Lane)
Robert Taylor and Frank McHugh, as songwriters, in *Her Cardboard Lover* (1942)

I DIDN'T KNOW WHAT TIME IT WAS (Rodgers–Hart)
Trudy Erwin, for Lucille Ball, in *Too Many Girls* (1940)

I DON'T WANT TO WALK WITHOUT YOU (Styne–Loesser)
Lizabeth Scott, as the nightclub thrush, in *Dark City* (1950)

I GET ALONG WITHOUT YOU VERY WELL (Carmichael–Thompson)
Jane Russell as the club singer, with pianist Hoagy Carmichael, initially in a flashback sequence, in *The Las Vegas Story* (1952)

I GUESS I'LL HAVE TO CHANGE MY PLAN (Schwartz–Dietz)
(extract) Kristy McNicoll and Marsha Mason in *Only When I Laugh* (UK: *It Hurts Only When I Laugh*) (1981)

I LOVE IT OUT HERE IN THE WEST (Spielman–Goell)
Ann Dvorak in *Abilene Town* (1946)

I MAY NEVER GO HOME AGAIN (Brooks–Roberts)
Marlene Dietrich, in the flashback scene, in *Witness For The Prosecution* (1958)

I WANNA BE LOVED BY YOU (Kalmar–Stothart–Ruby)
Marilyn Monroe in *Some Like It Hot* (1959)

I WONDER WHO'S KISSING HER NOW (Howard–Adams–Hough)
Cliff Edwards (formerly "Ukelele Ike") as he drives his trailer containing Barbara Stanwyck and Robert Young in *Red Salute* (also known as *Her Enlisted Man*) (1935)

I'LL GET BY (AS LONG AS I HAVE YOU) (Ahlert–Turk)
Irene Dunne to Spencer Tracy, with Ward Bond on harmonica, in *A Guy Named Joe* (1944)
(Irene sings it twice, after which Spencer Tracy plays an orchestral version on a jukebox, to which they both dance.)

I'LL REMEMBER APRIL (Raye–DePaul–Johnston)
Dick Foran in *Ride 'Em Cowboy* (1942)

I'LL TAKE YOU HOME AGAIN, KATHLEEN (Traditional)
The Sons Of The Pioneers in *Rio Grande* (1950)
(Played briefly by Irene Papas on the piano in *Tribute To A Badman* (1956) and on a bar-room piano in *Billy The Kid* (1941).)

I'M GETTIN' SENTIMENTAL OVER YOU (Bassman–Washington)
Carol Bruce in the Abbott And Costello comedy *Keep 'Em Flying* (1941)

I'M IN THE MOOD FOR LOVE (McHugh–Fields)
Gloria DeHaven in *Between Two Women* (1944)
Lizabeth Scott in *Dark City* (1950)
Dean Martin in *That's My Boy* (1951)
Shirley Booth in *About Mrs Leslie* (1954)

I'M JUST WILD ABOUT HARRY (Sissle–Blake)

Priscilla Lane in *The Roaring Twenties* (1939)

I'VE GOT A CRUSH ON YOU (George and Ira Gershwin)

Ellen Burstyn in *Alice Doesn't Live Here Anymore* (1974)

I'VE GOT YOU UNDER MY SKIN (Porter)

Tony Randall in *The Mating Game* (1959)

I'VE HEARD THAT SONG BEFORE (Styne–Cahn)

Edra Gale in *Farewell, My Lovely* (1975)

I'VE WRITTEN A LETTER TO DADDY (DeVol–Vincent–Jaffe–Tobias)

Bette Davis as Baby Jane Hudson, with Victor Buono as her pianist; also performed by Julie Alldred, acting the part of Jane as a young girl, in *Whatever Happened to Baby Jane* (1962)

ICH LIEBE DICH MY DEAR (Blight–Hart)

Gloria Swanson in *Perfect Understanding* (1933)

IF I COULD BE WITH YOU (ONE HOUR TONIGHT) (Creamer–Johnson)

Joan Crawford, briefly singing along with a radio, in *Flamingo Road* (1949)

IF YOU KNEW SUSIE (Meyer–DeSylva)

George Brent, Dennis O'Keefe, Don DeFore and Walter Abel, singing the praises of Joan Fontaine's character, in *The Affairs Of Susan* (1945)

IN MY ARMS (Loesser–Grouya)

Bob Crosby in *See Here, Private Hargrove* (1944)

IN THE GOOD OLD SUMMERTIME (Shields–Evans)

Oliver Hardy, accompanied by Stan Laurel on organ, performing as street musicians in a blinding snowstorm, in *Below Zero* (1930)

INKA DINKA DOO (Durante–Ryan)

Jimmy Durante in *Joe Palooka* (1934)

(Jimmy Durante sang it again in the 1944 musical *Two Girls And A Sailor*.)

ISN'T IT ROMANTIC (Rodgers–Hart)

Whistled by John Lund to Marlene Dietrich in *A Foreign Affair* (1948)

IT HAD BETTER BE TONIGHT (Mancini–Mercer)

Fran Jeffries in *The Pink Panther* (1964)

IT HAD TO BE YOU (Jones–Kahn)

Priscilla Lane, playing the part of James Cagney's protégée club singer, in *The Roaring Twenties* (1939)

Dooley Wilson as Sam in *Casablanca* (1943)

IT'S RAINING SUNBEAMS (Hollander–Coslow)

Deanna Durbin in *One Hundred Men And A Girl* (1937)

JEEPERS CREEPERS (Warren–Mercer)

Scatman Crothers, parodying Dooley Wilson's role of "Sam" in *Casablanca*, in *The Cheap Detective* (1978)

JINGLE, JANGLE, JINGLE (Lilley–Loesser)

Fred MacMurray, Paulette Goddard and a cowboy chorus in *Forest Rangers* (1942)

JONNY (Hollander–Heyman)

Marlene Dietrich, singing in a nightclub, in *Song Of Songs* (1933)

JUST A MOMENT MORE (Livingston–Evans)

Hedy Lamarr, singing in English

The jukebox plays the orchestral version of "I'll Get By" in *A Guy Named Joe* (1944), starring Spencer Tracy and Irene Dunne.

and French, in *My Favorite Spy* (1951)

LAZY MOON (Johnson–Cole)
Oliver Hardy (in black-face) in *Pardon Us* (1931)
LET ME CALL YOU SWEETHEART (Whitson–Friedman)

Oliver Hardy, serenading Della Lind, assisted by Stan Laurel playing the tuba, in *Swiss Miss* (1938)
LET'S FALL IN LOVE (Arlen–Koehler)
Don Ameche and Dorothy Lamour as a duet in *Slightly French* (1949)

Robert Cummings to Rosalind Russell in *Tell It To The Judge* (1949)

Judy Holliday and Jack Lemmon in *It Should Happen To You* (1954)

LISBON ANTIGUA (Portela–Dupree)
In English, by a studio chorus under the main titles and later, in Portuguese, by a female vocalist in a cafe scene, in *Lisbon* (1956)
(Nelson Riddle, who scored the film, successfully recorded "Lisbon Antigua" with his own orchestra, the single topping the American hit parade in 1956.)

LOUISE (Whiting–Robin)
Jerry Lewis in *The Stooge* (1952)
Maurice Chevalier in *A New Kind Of Love* (1963)
(One of Chevalier's most popular songs, he first sang it in the 1929 musical *Innocents Of Paris*. Another of his closely associated songs, "Mimi", is also sung by Chevalier in *A New Kind Of Love*.)

LOVE SONG OF THE NILE (Freed–Brown)
Ramon Novarro in *The Barbarian* (1933)

A LOVELY WAY TO SPEND AN EVENING (McHugh–Adamson)
Martha O'Driscoll in *Criminal Court* (1946)
Lizabeth Scott as a club singer in *The Racket* (1951)

LOVER (Rodgers–Hart)
Fred Astaire, as he tries to win back Lilli Palmer, in *The Pleasure Of His Company* (1961)

LOVERS WERE MEANT TO CRY (Brent)
Ava Gardner to Clark Gable in *Lone Star* (1952)

LYDIA, THE TATTOOED LADY (Arlen–Harburg)

Groucho Marx in *The Marx Brothers At The Circus* (1939)

MAMA GUITAR (Glazer–Shulberg)
Andy Griffith, as Lonesome Rhodes, the hillbilly singer who reaches frightening prominence, in *A Face In The Crowd* (1957)

MAMAS, DON'T LET YOUR BABIES GROW UP TO BE COWBOYS (E. and P. Bruce)
Willie Nelson in *The Electric Horseman* (1979)
Mickey Gilley and Johnny Lee in *Urban Cowboy* (1980)

THE MAN I LOVE (George and Ira Gershwin)
Peg LaCentra for Ida Lupino as the night club singer in *The Man I Love* (1946)

THE MAN ON THE FLYING TRAPEZE (O'Keefe)
Clark Gable and the bus passengers in *It Happened One Night* (1934)

LA MARSEILLAISE (France's National Anthem)
Paul Henreid, the resistance leader, with Corinna Mura and chorus in *Casablanca* (1943)
The French characters, in a spoof of the *Casablanca* sequence, in *The Cheap Detective* (1978)

MARY'S A GRAND OLD NAME (Cohan)
Charles Durning to Dustin Hoffman in *Tootsie* (1982)

THE MEANING OF THE BLUES (Troup–Worth)
Julie London, singing along with her own record broadcast over a radio, in *The Great Man* (1957)

A MELODY FROM THE SKY (Alter–Mitchell)
Fuzzy Knight, along with Henry Fonda whistling a few bars, in *The Trail Of The Lonesome Pine* (1936)

Robert Mitchum, a singer in his own right, strums a guitar with Loretta Young in *Rachel And The Stranger* (1948).

MEMPHIS IN JUNE (Carmichael–Webster)
> Hoagy Carmichael in *Johnny Angel* (1945)

MOANIN' LOW (Rainger–Dietz)
> Claire Trevor, goaded by Edward G. Robinson, in *Key Largo* (1948)

MONEY (THAT'S WHAT I WANT) (Gordy–Bradford)
> John Belushi in *National Lampoon's Animal House* (1978)

MOON RIVER (Mancini–Mercer)
> Audrey Hepburn, sitting on a fire escape strumming a guitar, in *Breakfast At Tiffany's* (1961)

MULE TRAIN (Glickman–Lange–Heath)
> Vaughn Monroe in *Singing Guns* (1950)
> Gene Autry in *Mule Train* (1950)

MULTIPLICATION (Darin)
> Bobby Darin in *Come September* (1961)

MY DREAMS ARE GETTING BETTER ALL THE TIME (Mizzy–Curtis)
> Marion Hutton in the Abbott And Costello comedy *In Society* (1944)

MY RESISTANCE IS LOW (Tucker)
> Jane Russell in *The Las Vegas Story* (1952)

MY RIFLE, MY PONY AND ME (Tiomkin–Webster)
> Dean Martin and Ricky Nelson in *Rio Bravo* (1959)

NEARER MY GOD TO THEE (Traditional)
> Clifton Webb and the male passengers, as the ship sinks, in *Titanic* (1953)

NIGHT AND DAY (Porter)
Deanna Durbin in *Lady On A Train* (1946)

NO LOVE, NO NOTHIN' (Warren–Robin)
Jane Russell, entertaining the troops, in *Fate Is The Hunter* (1964)
(Song first sung by Alice Faye in the 1943 musical *The Gang's All Here*.)

NOW YOU SEE IT, NOW YOU DON'T (Loesser–Press)
Veronica Lake, as the singing magician, before an audience that includes Laird Cregar, in *This Gun For Hire* (1942)

O-HE-O-HI-O-HO (Webb–Salt)
Robert Mitchum, strumming a guitar, as he strolls towards William Holden's farm, in *Rachel And The Stranger* (1948)

THE OBJECT OF MY AFFECTION (Tomlin–Poe–Grier)
Pinky Tomlin in *Times Square Lady* (1935)

OH, GIVE ME TIME FOR TENDERNESS (Goulding–Janis)
Vera Van, with (briefly) Bette Davis, in *Dark Victory* (1939)

OLD MAN MOON (Carmichael)
Hoagy Carmichael, aided by Cary Grant and Constance Bennett, in *Topper* (1937)

OLE BUTTERMILK SKY (Carmichael–Brooks) Hoagy Carmichael in *Canyon Passage* (1946)

ON THE GOOD SHIP LOLLIPOP (Whiting–Clare)
Shirley Temple, on board a plane with a seemingly endless runway, in *Bright Eyes* (1934)

ONE DAY SINCE YESTERDAY (Ball–Bogdanovich)
Colleen Camp in *They All Laughed* (1981)

ONE FOR MY BABY (AND ONE MORE FOR THE ROAD) (Arlen–Mercer)
Ida Lupino in *Road House* (1948)
Jane Russell in *Macao* (1952)

OTCHI TCHORNIYA (Salama)
Gloria Jean in *Never Give A Sucker An Even Break* (1941)
(The Russian folk song was also sung by Al Jolson in his 1934 musical *Wonder Bar*, performed as a veritable tongue twister by Danny Kaye in 1945's *Wonder Man*, and parodied by Spike Jones And His City Slickers as "Hotcha Cornia" in the 1943 extravaganza *Thank Your Lucky Stars*.)
(See "Dark Eyes" in "Movie Musical Songs".)

OVER THE RAINBOW (Arlen–Harburg)
James Stewart in *The Philadelphia Story* (1940)

OVER YOU (Roberts–Hart)
Betty Buckley in *Tender Mercies* (1983)

PARADISE (Brown–Clifford)
Pola Negri in *A Woman Commands* (1929)
Belita in *The Gangster* (1947)
Gloria Grahame in *A Woman's Secret* (1949)
Valentina Cortese in *Malaya* (1949)

PLEASE (Rainger–Robin)
Jack Oakie in *From Hell To Heaven* (1933)

PLEASE DON'T TALK ABOUT ME WHEN I'M GONE (Clare–Stept)
Patricia Neal in *The Breaking Point* (1950)

PRETTY LITTLE GIRL IN THE YELLOW DRESS (Tiomkin–Washington)
Kirk Douglas to Carol Lynley in *The Last Sunset* (1961)

Jane Russell singing "You Kill Me", which was specially written for *Macao* (1952).

PUT THE BLAME ON MAME (Fisher–Roberts)
Anita Ellis for Rita Hayworth as the seductive songstress in *Gilda* (1946)
Jean Porter, with Jan Savitt And His Orchestra, in *Betty Co-Ed* (1947)
PUTTIN' ON THE RITZ (Berlin)
Clark Gable in *Idiot's Delight* (1939)
Gene Wilder and Peter Boyle in *Young Frankenstein* (1974)

QUE SERA, SERA (see WHATEVER WILL BE, WILL BE)

RALLY ROUND THE FLAG BOYS (Traditional)
Miriam Hopkins, as a dance-hall singer, in *Virginia City* (1940)
RATHER HAVE THE BLUES (DeVol)
Madi Comfort, the nightclub singer, in *Kiss Me Deadly* (1955)
(The same song was sung behind the main titles by Nat "King" Cole.)
RED RIVER VALLEY (Traditional)
Henry Fonda, while dancing with Jane Darwell, in *The Grapes Of Wrath* (1940)
(Tune is heard throughout the film, either orchestrally or by a solo accordion.)
RING OF FIRE (Carter–Kilgore)
Blondie in *Roadie* (1980)
ROUND AND ROUND (Lange–Stewart)
Gary Cooper, riding on horseback, alongside William De-

Anita Ellis supplied the voice for sultry Rita Hayworth when she sang "Put The Blame On Mame" in the 1946 movie *Gilda*.

There *NEVER* was a woman like Gilda!

COLUMBIA PICTURES presents

RITA HAYWORTH as

Gilda

with

GLENN FORD

GEORGE MACREADY
JOSEPH CALLEIA

Screenplay by Marion Parsonnet
Produced by VIRGINIA VAN UPP
Directed by CHARLES VIDOR

Great as is her powerful dramatic portrayal—great, too, is this dancing Hayworth—singing "Put the Blame on Mame"!

marest, in *Along Came Jones* (1945)

RUNNIN' WILD (Gibbs–Bray–Wood)
Marilyn Monroe, fronting the all-girl orchestra on board train, in *Some Like It Hot* (1959)

SADDLE THE WIND (Livingston–Evans)
Julie London to John Cassavetes in *Saddle The Wind* (1958)

SAY NO MORE, IT'S GOODBYE (Auric–Langdon)
Diahann Carroll to Anthony Perkins in *Goodbye Again* (1961)
(For *Goodbye Again* — the film based on the novel *Aimez Vous Brahms* — Georges Auric adapted a Brahms melody for the main theme of the picture.)

SEE WHAT THE BOYS IN THE BACKROOM WILL HAVE (see THE BOYS IN THE BACKROOM)

SEEMS LIKE OLD TIMES (Lombardo–Loeb)
Diane Keaton in *Annie Hall* (1977)

SILENT NIGHT (Traditional)
Christmas carol heard in countless pictures, but particularly memorable as sung by Dorothy Lamour in *Donovan's Reef* (1963)

SILVER BELLS (Livingston–Evans)
Bob Hope and Marilyn Maxwell in *The Lemon Drop Kid* (1951)

SMOKE DREAMS (Brown–Freed)
Dorothy McNulty (later known as Penny Singleton) in *After The Thin Man* (1934)
(In the same scene — a surprise party for Nick and Nora — the Louis Prima song "Sing, Sing, Sing" is also featured.)

SO MUCH TO ME (Tiomkin–Jones)
Helen Humes, in a New Orleans Club, in *The Steel Trap* (1952)

SOME SUNDAY MORNING (Heindorf–Jerome–Koehler)
Alexis Smith, as the singing actress, in *San Antonio* (1945)

SOMETHING TO REMEMBER YOU BY (Schwartz–Dietz)
Janis Paige in *Her Kind Of Man* (1946)

SOMETHING'S GOTTA GIVE (Mercer)
Joanne Woodward in *The Stripper* (1963)

SPIN A LITTLE WEB OF DREAMS (Fain–Kahal)
Verree Teasdale and chorus in a lavish Busby Berkeley routine (famed for its "Hall Of Human Harps" tableau) in *Fashions Of 1934* (1934)

SPRING WILL BE A LITTLE LATE THIS YEAR (Loesser)
Deanna Durbin in *Christmas Holiday* (1944)

SPRINGTIME FOR HITLER (Brooks)
Chorus in *The Producers* (1967)

STRANGER IN PARADISE (Borodin–Wright–Forrest)
Buck Henry, the drunken parent, in *Taking Off* (1971)

SWEET ADELINE (Armstrong–Gerard)
The Four Marx Brothers, as they hide in individual herring barrels, at the opening of *Monkey Business* (1931)

SWEET GEORGIA BROWN (Bernie–Pinkard–Casey)
Mel Brooks and Anne Bancroft (singing in Polish) in *To Be Or Not To Be* (1983)

TAKE IT OFF THE E-STRING, PLAY IT ON THE G-STRING (Akst–Cahn)
Barbara Stanwyck, singing and stripping, as Dixie Daisy in *Lady Of Burlesque* (UK: *Striptease Lady*) (1943)

TAKING A CHANCE ON LOVE (Duke–Latouche–Fetter)
Dorothy Dandridge in *Remains To Be Seen* (1953)

TAMMY (Livingston–Evans)

Debbie Reynolds in *Tammy And The Bachelor* (UK: *Tammy*) (1957)
Sandra Dee in *Tammy And The Doctor* (1963)
(Song was actually first heard in *Tammy And The Bachelor* sung under the main titles by The Ames Brothers.)

TENEMENT SYMPHONY (Borne–Kuller–Golden)
Tony Martin in *The Big Store* (1941)

THAT OLD BLACK MAGIC (Arlen–Mercer)
Lizabeth Scott in *Dark City* (1950)
Marilyn Monroe in *Bus Stop* (1956)

THAT'S AMORE (Warren–Brooks)
Dean Martin in *The Caddy* (1953)

THAT'S LOVE (Rodgers–Hart)
Anna Sten, vocalising in the Dietrich manner, in *Nana* (1934)

THERE'LL BE SOME CHANGES MADE (Overstreet–Higgins)
Ida Lupino in *Road House* (1948)
Joan Blondell in *The Blue Veil* (1951)
Dolores Gray in *Designing Woman* (1957)

THEY DIDN'T BELIEVE ME (Kern–Reynolds)
Vanessa Redgrave in *Agatha* (1978)

THIS OLD MAN (see THE CHILDREN'S MARCHING SONG)

THIS YEAR (Keating)
Carmen McRae, in a nightclub sequence, in *Hotel* (1967)

TOOT, TOOT, TOOTSIE, GOODBYE (Russo–Kahn–Erdman)
June Allyson and Van Johnson in *Remains To Be Seen* (1953)
(Song particularly associated with Al Jolson — see "Movie Musical Songs" — and played briefly by

Stan Laurel nurses the pineapples as Oliver Hardy sings "Honolulu Baby" in *Sons Of The Desert* (1933). Their 1975 British hit, "Trail Of The Lonesome Pine", recorded in 1937, unofficially holds the record for the oldest recording ever to achieve Top Ten status.

Hoagy Carmichael in *The Best Years Of Our Lives*.)

TRAIL OF THE LONESOME PINE (Carroll–MacDonald)
Laurel And Hardy, backed up by The Avalon Boys featuring Chill Wills, in *Way Out West* (1937)

TUMBLING TUMBLEWEEDS (Nolan)
Gene Autry in *Tumbling Tumbleweeds* (1935)
Roy Rogers in *Silver Spurs* (1943)
(The Sons Of The Pioneers, including Bob Nolan himself, sang this in 1944's *Hollywood Canteen*.)

TWILIGHT ON THE TRAIL (Alter–Mitchell)
Fuzzy Knight, aided by Nigel Bruce humming and Fred Mac-

Murray whistling, in *The Trail Of The Lonesome Pine* (1936)

A VERY PRECIOUS LOVE (Fain–Webster)
Gene Kelly in *Marjorie Morningstar* (1958)

LA VIE EN ROSE (Loviguy–Piaf)
Audrey Hepburn to Humphrey Bogart in *Sabrina* (UK: *Sabrina Fair*) (1954)

WE MAY NEVER LOVE LIKE THIS AGAIN (Kasha–Hirschorn)
Maureen McGovern in *Towering Inferno* (1974)

WHAT AM I BID FOR MY APPLES? (Hajos–Robin)

Marlene Dietrich, the cabaret singer, to Gary Cooper, the legionnaire, in *Morocco* (1930)

WHAT IS THIS THING CALLED LOVE (Porter)
Peg LaCentra, the nightclub singer, aptly punctuating Joan Crawford's dialogue, in *Humoresque* (1947)

WHATEVER WILL BE, WILL BE (QUE SERA, SERA) (Livingston–Evans)
Doris Day in *The Man Who Knew Too Much* (1956)
Also featured by Doris Day in two of her later movies: *Please Don't Eat The Daisies* (1960) and *The Glass Bottom Boat* (1966), and utilised as the theme for her 1968–73 television series.

WHEN I FALL IN LOVE (Young–Heyman)
Nat "King" Cole in *Istanbul* (1957) (Song based on the recurring theme in the 1952 movie *One Minute To Zero*.)

WHERE OR WHEN (Rodgers–Hart)
Gloria Wood, in a club sequence, in *Gaby* (1956)

THE WHIPPOORWILL (Raye–Mitchum)
Keely Smith in *Thunder Road* (1958)

WHISKEY HEAVEN (Crofford–Durrill–Garrett)
Fats Domino in *Any Which Way You Can* (1980)

WHO ARE WE TO SAY (Wells–Karger)
Peggy Ryan and Ray MacDonald in *All Ashore* (1953)

WHO CARES WHAT PEOPLE SAY (Jerome–Scholl)
Ann Sheridan, a nightclub singer, with Kent Smith in the audience, in *Nora Prentiss* (1947)

WHO KNOWS (Revel–Greene)

Martha Mears for Lucille Ball with Ozzie Nelson And His Orchestra in *The Big Street* (1942)

WILLOW WEEP FOR ME (Ronell)
Marion Hutton in *Love Happy* (1950)

WISH ME A RAINBOW (Livingston–Evans)
Natalie Wood and Mary Badham in *This Property Is Condemned* (1966)

WISHING (DeSylva)
A trio of young girls with ukulele accompaniment in *Love Affair* (1939)
(Song later featured in the 1945 musical *George White's Scandals*.)

WON'T SOMEBODY DANCE WITH ME (DePaul)
Diana Quick in *The Big Sleep* (1977)

YOU ARE MY SUNSHINE (Davis)
Tex Ritter in *Take Me Back To Old Oklahoma* (1940)

YOU BELONG TO ME (David–Rose)
Steve Martin and Bernadette Peters in *The Jerk* (1979)

YOU BOTHER ME AN AWFUL LOT (Fain–Kahal)
Ann Dvorak in a club sequence in *G-Men* (1935)

YOU CAME A LONG WAY FROM ST. LOUIS (Russell–Brooks)
Peggy King in *Abbott And Costello Meet The Mummy* (1955)

YOU CAME ALONG (FROM OUT OF NOWHERE) (Green–Heyman)
Helen Forrest in *You Came Along* (1945)

YOU DO SOMETHING TO ME (Porter)
Peg LaCentra, the nightclub singer, with (briefly) Joan Crawford, in *Humoresque* (1947)

YOU MUST HAVE BEEN A BEAUTIFUL BABY (Warren–Mercer)

"You Came Along", featured in the 1945 movie of the same name, was sung by Helen Forrest.

Dick Powell to Olivia De Havilland in *Hard To Get* (1938)
YOU'RE GONNA HEAR FROM ME (Previn–Langdon)
Jackie Ward for Natalie Wood in *Inside Daisy Clover* (1965)
YOU'RE THE TOP (Porter)
Diana Rigg in *Evil Under The Sun* (1981)

ZING! WENT THE STRINGS OF MY HEART (Hanley)
Judy Garland in *Listen, Darling* (1938)
ZIP-A-DEE-DOO-DAH (Wrubel–Gilbert)
James Baskett in *Song Of The South* (1948)

18 WHO SANG WHAT FOR WHOM

On various occasions, when actors burst into song on the screen, what comes out of their mouths is not always their own voice, which brings us to the gentle art of dubbing.

Quoting well-recognised cases, certain listings in this book indicate that, for instance, Jane Froman sang for Susan Hayward, but Hollywood has usually seen fit not to reveal who "ghosted" such vocals.

The term "dubbing" does not just apply to vocal performers, for movies have long "ghosted" instrumentalists, such as Leonard Pennario playing piano for Louis Jourdan in 1956's *Julie*, and Harry James playing the trumpet solos for Kirk Douglas in 1950's *Young Man With A Horn*.

Similarly, actors have, from time to time, been provided with voice stand-ins. For example, 1957's *Run Of The Arrow*, when Angie Dickinson dubbed Spanish actress Sarita Montiel; and for a gag, at the close of 1946's *Never Say Goodbye*, Errol Flynn adopts the voice of a tough guy by means of the off-screen assistance of Humphrey Bogart himself.

Of all the singing actresses from the golden years, Rita Hayworth was dubbed on probably more occasions than anyone else, and the identities of her stand-in vocalists are widely known.

Anita Ellis sang for her in 1946's *Gilda* and 1947's *Down To Earth*; Nan Wynn did the honours in 1942's *My Gal Sal*; Martha Mears in 1945's *Tonight And Every Night*; and it was Jo Ann Greer who ghosted for Rita in 1952's

Affair In Trinidad, 1953's *Miss Sadie Thompson*, and the 1957 musical *Pal Joey*, in which her big numbers were "Zip" and "Bewitched". Soundtrack albums invariably kept this kind of secret, and the *Pal Joey* record contains nothing to indicate an alternative singer.

It is by no means certain that if a performer is dubbed on one occasion,

Jo Ann Greer, one of Rita Hayworth's off-screen voices, was a band singer in her own right with Les Brown and his Band of Renown.

they did not actually sing on others. For example, in 1948's *Road House*, after Ida Lupino finishes her first song, Celeste Holm cracks: "She does more without a voice than anybody I've ever heard!" which is a realistic comment, because while never a great singer, Miss Lupino's vocal attributes were perfectly suited to the character of Chicago entertainer Lily Stevens, contrasting with her nightclub thrush in 1947's *The Man I Love*, for which she was dubbed by Peg LaCentra, a full-fledged singer in her own right, and a one-time vocalist with Artie Shaw.

It is, at times, quite possible to detect when an actor is not using his or her own voice, as in 1952's *Moulin Rouge*, when Zsa Zsa Gabor, as a music-hall singer befriended by Toulouse-Lautrec, is obviously and poorly dubbed, "singing" "Where Is Your Heart" (Auric–Engvick), particularly as the adopted voice appears distantly related to the actress's natural tone.

A particularly intriguing case of Hollywood voice substitution concerns Joan Blondell who, as far as I know, really did sing "Daddy" (Troup) in 1951's *The Blue Veil*, a sequence incidentally for which an uncredited Busby Berkeley was brought in to direct. However, some years before, in the musical *Gold Diggers Of 1933*, Joan was the key performer in the film's closing number, "Remember My Forgotten Man". The opening verse and first chorus is spoken by Miss Blondell, after which Etta Moten (whose rich voice adorned "The Carioca" number in 1933's *Flying Down To Rio*) takes up a repeat chorus as she herself is pictured, sitting in the framework of a window. The Busby Berkeley-staged sequence then moves into high gear and a full studio chorus

repeats another chorus of the song. However, the whole number climaxes with Joan Blondell reappearing and "singing" the final portion with outstretched arms, but she is actually miming to Etta Moten's voice.

Here are a few of the other known and much-discussed occasions when voices off-camera provided vocals for performers on-screen:

EDDIE CANTOR provided his own vocals for Keefe Brasselle, who portrayed him in 1953's *The Eddie Cantor Story*.

KASEY CISYK for Didi Conn, singing the title song (Brooks) in 1977's *You Light Up My Life*, later covered on record by Debby Boone.

BUDDY CLARK was the real owner of Jack Haley's first-rate vocal chords in 1937's *Wake Up And Live*.

BING CROSBY made it possible for Eddie Bracken to convincingly play a Western Union messenger who could croon in 1945's *Out Of This World*.

BURTON CUMMINGS sang the title song (Webb) and two other numbers for Michael Ontkean, as the nightclub singer, in 1979's *Voices*.

ANITA ELLIS actually sang "Put The Blame On Mame" (Fisher–Roberts) for Rita Hayworth in 1946's *Gilda*, and also provided the voice double for Vera-Ellen in 1950's *Three Little Words*.

CONNIE FRANCIS sang for Tuesday Weld in 1957's *Rock, Rock, Rock*.

JANE FROMAN sang her own songs as Susan Hayward portrayed her character in 1952's *With A Song In My Heart*.

GOGI GRANT ghosted all the vocals

for Ann Blyth as Helen Morgan in 1957's *The Helen Morgan Story* (UK: *Both Ends Of The Candle*).

LOUANNE HOGAN sang "It Might As Well Be Spring" (Rodgers–Hammerstein) in 1945's *State Fair*, and "In Love In Vain" (Kern–Robin) in 1946's *Centennial Summer*, both for Jeanne Crain.

AL JOLSON sang all his songs on the soundtracks, while Larry Parks portrayed him on-screen in both 1946's *The Jolson Story* and 1949's *Jolson Sings Again*.

ALLAN JONES actually sang "A Pretty Girl Is Like A Melody" (Berlin) for an unusually silent Dennis Morgan in 1936's *The Great Ziegfeld*.

PEG LACENTRA sang the title number and other songs for Ida Lupino in 1947's *The Man I Love*, as well as the vocals for Susan Hayward in 1947's *Smash Up: The Story Of A Woman*.

MARIO LANZA sang for Edmund Purdom as Prince Karl in 1954's *The Student Prince*.

MARNI NIXON aided Deborah Kerr in 1956's *The King And I*. She also dubbed for Natalie Wood in 1962's *Gypsy* and 1961's *West Side Story*, and for Audrey Hepburn in 1964's *My Fair Lady*.

GIORGIO TOZZI sang for Rossano Brazzi in 1958's *South Pacific*.

VIRGINIA VERRILL sang both "Did I Remember" (Adamson–Donaldson) in 1936's *Suzy*, as well as the title song (Kern–Hammerstein) in 1935's *Reckless*, both for Jean Harlow.

MARGARET WHITING sang "I'll Plant My Own Tree" (A. and D. Previn) for Susan Hayward in 1967's *Valley Of The Dolls*.

EILEEN WILSON provided "Don't Tell Me" (Pepper) in 1947's *The Hucksters* for Ava Gardner, and "Speak Low" (Weill–Nash) in 1948's *One Touch Of Venus* which Miss Gardner sang to Dick Haymes; though supposedly it really was Ava Gardner singing "The More I Know Of Love" (Rozsa–Brooks) as Burt Lancaster looks on, in 1946's *The Killers*.

Of all the dubbing legends, the one that a very young Andy Williams provided for Lauren Bacall in 1944's *To Have And Have Not* persists undaunted, though it is probably the hardest to believe.

The art of voice substitution remains intriguing and, hopefully, a complete book on the subject will be forthcoming. Until then we must be content with the realisation that this portion of film-making is not all that it seems, which after all, is in keeping with other elements of cinematic fantasy.

Before closing this section, mention should be made of one of the movies that pictorially satirises voice dubbing.

In 1952's *Singin' In The Rain*, Jean Hagen plays a silent star whose career is severely threatened as sound movies begin, and her shrill, coarse voice is obviously a liability. So the studio hires Debbie Reynolds to sing for her, but the secret is suddenly and embarrassingly revealed at a personal appearance, when Hagen on centre-stage is miming to Reynolds, who is masked by just a single curtain which is mistakenly opened in mid-song!

One final point worth noting is that in 1950's *Three Little Words*, Debbie Reynolds portrayed the "boop-boop-a-doop" girl, Helen Kane, and for the song, "I Wanna Be Loved By

Helen Kane, the lady with the petite voice, created her reputation as the "boop-boop-a-doop girl". She dubbed for Debbie Reynolds in *Three Little Words* (1950).

You" (Ruby–Stothart–Kalmar), Miss Reynolds mimed to Helen Kane's voice.

19 MOVIE MUSICAL SONGS

The final section is devoted to a representative catalogue of outstanding movie musical songs. As elsewhere in this book, the majority of entries are from Hollywood productions, with a sprinkling of other sources represented plus some key numbers from rock movies. Like the musicals themselves, the sequences chosen cover a diverse range of styles and performers. To suggest the broad scope covered, consider the evolution of early sound musicals recorded with live musicians on stage prior to the playback system — Mae West posing the loaded question "(I Wonder Where My) Easy Rider's Gone" (Brooks) in 1933's *She Done Him Wrong*, the elegance of Fred Astaire and Eleanor Powell dancing as Douglas McPhail sings Cole Porter's "I Concentrate On You" in *The Broadway Melody Of 1940*, sultry Lena Horne singing "Paper Doll" (Black) in 1944's *Two Girls And A Sailor*, through to such contemporary items as Gene Wilder accounting for his self-description, "The Candy Man" (Bricusse–Newley) in 1971's *Willy Wonka And The Chocolate Factory*, Liza Minnelli and Joel Grey in one of the highlights from 1972's *Cabaret* namely "Money, Money" (Kander–Ebb), Rose Royce on the soundtrack, leading us into the first notable disco sequence, the title number from 1976's *Car Wash* (Whitfield), Ren Woods supported by the company in the 1979 film of *Hair!*, Aretha Franklin struttin' her stuff, recreating her 1968 hit "Think" (Franklin–White) in 1980's *The Blues Brothers* and, finally, the combination of Dolly Parton and Burt Reynolds, performing "Sneakin' Around" (Parton) from the 1982 adaptation (with additional songs) of *The Best Little Whorehouse In Texas*.

ABA DABA HONEYMOON (Donovan–Fields)
Debbie Reynolds and Carleton Carpenter in *Two Weeks With Love* (1950)

ABOUT A QUARTER TO NINE (Warren–Dubin)
Al Jolson, with Ruby Keeler dancing, in *Go Into Your Dance* (UK: *Casino De Paris*) (1935)
Al Jolson for Larry Parks as Al Jolson in *The Jolson Story* (1946)

AC-CENT-TCHU-ATE THE POSITIVE (Arlen–Mercer)
Bing Crosby in *Here Come The Waves* (1944)

ACID QUEEN (Townshend)
Tina Turner in *Tommy* (1975)

Ruby Keeler and Al Jolson look to the stars in *Go Into Your Dance* (1935).

Alice Faye sings Irving Berlin's title song in the opening number from *Alexander's Ragtime Band* (1938). Accompanying her are Tyrone Power on violin and Jack Haley on drums.

AIN'T MISBEHAVIN' (Waller–Brooks)
Fats Waller in *Stormy Weather* (1943)
Louis Armstrong in *Atlantic City* (1944)

ALEXANDER'S RAGTIME BAND (Berlin)
Alice Faye in *Alexander's Ragtime Band* (1938)

ALL BY MYSELF (Berlin)
Bing Crosby in *Blue Skies* (1946)

ALL I DO IS DREAM OF YOU (Brown–Freed)
Gene Kelly and Debbie Reynolds in *Singin' In The Rain* (1952)
Debbie Reynolds and Bobby Van in *Affairs Of Dobie Gillis* (1953)
Twiggy to Christopher Gable in *The Boy Friend* (1971)

ALL OF ME (Marks–Simons)
Frank Sinatra in *Meet Danny Wilson* (1952)

ALL OF YOU (Porter)
Fred Astaire to Cyd Charisse in *Silk Stockings* (1957)

ALL THE WAY (Van Heusen–Cahn)
Frank Sinatra as Joe E. Lewis in *The Joker Is Wild* (1957)

ALL'S FAIR IN LOVE AND WAR (Warren–Dubin)
Dick Powell, Joan Blondell, Lee Dixon and Rosalind Marquis in *Gold Diggers of 1937* (1937)

AM I BLUE (Akst–Clarke)
Ethel Waters in *On With The Show* (1929)
Barbra Streisand in *Funny Lady* (1975)

AN AMERICAN TRILOGY (Newbury)
Ronnie McDowell for Kurt Russell as Elvis Presley in *Elvis* (1979 television movie, released theatrically as *Elvis — The Movie*)

AND THE ANGELS SING (Elman–Mercer)
Betty Hutton, Dorothy Lamour, Fred MacMurray, Mimi Chandler and Diana Lynn in *And The Angels Sing* (1943)
Martha Tilton and Benny Goodman And His Orchestra in *The*

Benny Goodman Story (1956)

AND THIS IS MY BELOVED (Wright–Forrest)
Howard Keel, Ann Blyth and Vic Damone in *Kismet* (1955)

ANIMAL CRACKERS IN MY SOUP (Koehler–Caesar)
Shirley Temple in *Curly Top* (1935)

ANYTHING GOES (Porter)
Ethel Merman in *Anything Goes* (1936)
Mitzi Gaynor in *Anything Goes* (1956)

ANYTHING YOU CAN DO, I CAN DO BETTER (Berlin)
Betty Hutton and Howard Keel in *Annie Get Your Gun* (1950)

APRIL IN PARIS (Duke–Harburg)
Doris Day in *April In Paris* (1953)

APRIL LOVE (Fain–Webster)
Pat Boone and Shirley Jones in *April Love* (1957)

APRIL SHOWERS (Silvers–DeSylva)
Al Jolson for Larry Parks in *The Jolson Story* (1946)
Jack Carson and Ann Sothern in *April Showers* (1948)

ARTHUR MURRAY TAUGHT ME DANCING IN A HURRY (Schertzinger–Mercer)
Betty Hutton in *The Fleet's In* (1942)

AS LONG AS THERE'S MUSIC (Styne–Cahn)
Frank Sinatra in *Step Lively* (1944)

AT LAST (Warren Gordon)
Glenn Miller And His Orchestra in *Sun Valley Serenade* (1941)
Glenn Miller And His Orchestra in *Orchestra Wives* (1942)

BABY FACE (Akst–Davis)
Al Jolson for Larry Parks in *Jolson Sings Again* (1949)

BABY, IT'S COLD OUTSIDE (Loesser) Ricardo Montalban and

The Blonde Bombshell, Betty Hutton, as Annie Oakley in *Annie Get Your Gun* (1950). She later made a comeback, touring in the road company of the Strouse-Charnin musical, *Annie*.

Esther Williams in *Neptune's Daughter* (1949)

BABY, TAKE A BOW (Gorney–Brown)
Shirley Temple and James Dunn in *Stand Up And Cheer* (1934)

BAUBLES, BANGLES AND BEADS (Wright–Forrest)
Ann Blyth in *Kismet* (1955)

BE A CLOWN (Porter)
Judy Garland and Gene Kelly in *The Pirate* (1948)

Fred Astaire and Eleanor Powell with their brilliant "Begin The Beguine" routine from the *Broadway Melody Of 1940* (1940).

BE MY LOVE (Brodsky–Cahn)
Mario Lanza and Kathryn Grayson in *Toast Of New Orleans* (1950)

BEGIN THE BEGUINE (Porter)
Studio Chorus accompanying the dancing of Fred Astaire and Eleanor Powell in *Broadway Melody Of 1940* (1940)
Carlos Ramirez in *Night And Day* (1946)

BEND DOWN SISTER (Conrad–Silverstein)
Charlotte Greenwood in *Palmy Days* (1931)

THE BEST THINGS IN LIFE ARE FREE (DeSylva–Brown–Henderson)
June Allyson and Peter Lawford in *Good News* (1947)
Gordon MacRae, Sheree North, Dan Dailey and Ernest Borgnine in *The Best Things In Life Are Free* (1956)

BEWITCHED (Rodgers–Hart)
Frank Sinatra and Jo Ann Greer for Rita Hayworth in *Pal Joey* (1957)

BEYOND THE BLUE HORIZON (Harling–Whiting)
Jeanette MacDonald in *Monte Carlo* (1930)
Jeanette MacDonald in *Follow The Boys* (1944)

BIDIN' MY TIME (George and Ira Gershwin)
Judy Garland and The King's Men in *Girl Crazy* (1943)

BIG SPENDER (Coleman–Fields)
Shirley MacLaine and Chita Rivera in *Sweet Charity* (1968)

BILL (Kern–Wodehouse)
Helen Morgan in *Show Boat* (1936)
Annette Warren for Ava Gardner in *Show Boat* (1951)
Gogi Grant for Ann Blyth as Helen Morgan in *The Helen Morgan Story* (UK: *Both Ends Of The Candle*) (1957)

THE BIRTH OF THE BLUES (DeSylva–Brown–Henderson)
Bing Crosby in *Birth Of The Blues* (1941)

Danny Thomas in *The Jazz Singer* (1953)

Gordon MacRae in *The Best Things In Life Are Free* (1956)

BLESS YOUR BEAUTIFUL HIDE (DePaul–Mercer)

Howard Keel in *Seven Brides For Seven Brothers* (1954)

BLUE HAWAII (Rainger–Robin)

Bing Crosby in *Waikiki Wedding* (1937)

Elvis Presley in *Blue Hawaii* (1961)

BLUE MOON (Rodgers–Hart)

Mel Torme in *Words And Music* (1948)

Jane Froman for Susan Hayward as Jane Froman in *With A Song In My Heart* (1952)

Robert DeNiro and Mary Kay Place in *New York, New York* (1977)

Sha Na Na in *Grease* (1978)

BLUE SKIES (Berlin)

Eddie Cantor in *Glorifying The American Girl* (1929)

Alice Faye and Ethel Merman in *Alexander's Ragtime Band* (1938)

Al Jolson in *The Jazz Singer* (1927)

Bing Crosby in *Blue Skies* (1946)

Bing Crosby and Danny Kaye in *White Christmas* (1954)

BLUES IN THE NIGHT (Arlen–Mercer)

Uncredited vocalist and Jimmy Lunceford And His Orchestra in *Blues In The Night* (1941)

John Garfield, in a comedy routine, in *Thank Your Lucky Stars* (1943)

BORN IN A TRUNK (Arlen–Gershwin)

Judy Garland (with interruptions from a voice provided off-screen by Humphrey Bogart saying "Sing Melancholy Baby") in *A Star Is Born* (1954)

BOSOM BUDDIES (Herman)

Mel Torme in *Words And Music* (1948).

Lucille Ball and Beatrice Arthur in *Mame* (1974)

THE BOY NEXT DOOR (Martin–Blane)

Judy Garland, singing of Tom Drake, in *Meet Me In St. Louis* (1944)

BROADWAY MELODY (Brown–Freed)

Charles King in *Broadway Melody* (1929)

Gene Kelly in *Singin' In The Rain* (1952)

101

BROADWAY RHYTHM (Rodgers–Hart)
Frances Langford in *Broadway Melody Of 1936* (1935)
Judy Garland in *Babes In Arms* (1939)
Judy Garland, briefly, in *Presenting Lily Mars* (1943)
Gene Kelly in *Singin' In The Rain* (1952)

BROTHERHOOD OF MAN (Loesser)
Robert Morse and Rudy Vallee in *How To Succeed In Business Without Really Trying* (1967)

BUSY DOING NOTHING (Van Heusen–Burke)
Bing Crosby, William Bendix and Cedric Hardwicke in *A Connecticut Yankee* (UK: *A Connecticut Yankee In King Arthur's Court*) (1949)

BUT NOT FOR ME (George and Ira Gershwin)
Judy Garland in *Girl Crazy* (1943)
Harve Presnell and Connie Francis in *Girl Crazy* (UK: *When The Boys Meet The Girls*) (1966)

BUTTON UP YOUR OVERCOAT (DeSylva–Brown–Henderson)
Gordon MacRae, Sheree North, Dan Dailey and Ernest Borgnine in *The Best Things In Life Are Free* (1956)

BY A WATERFALL (Fain–Kahal)
Dick Powell and Ruby Keeler in *Footlight Parade* (1933)

BY MYSELF (Schwartz–Dietz)
Fred Astaire in *The Band Wagon* (1953)

BY THE LIGHT OF THE SILVERY MOON (Edwards–Madden)
Bing Crosby in *Birth Of The Blues* (1941)
Scotty Beckett in *The Jolson Story* (1946)
Doris Day and Gordon MacRae in *By The Light Of The Silvery Moon* (1953)

BYE, BYE, BABY (Styne–Robin)
Marilyn Monroe and Jane Russell in *Gentlemen Prefer Blondes* (1953)

BYE, BYE LOVE (F. and B. Bryant)
Ben Vereen and Roy Scheider in *All That Jazz* (1979)

CABARET (Kander–Ebb)
Liza Minnelli in *Cabaret* (1972)

CALIFORNIA HERE I COME (Jolson–DeSylva–Meyer)
Al Jolson in *Rose Of Washington Square* (1939)
Al Jolson for Larry Parks in *The Jolson Story* (1946)
Jane Froman for Susan Hayward in *With A Song In My Heart* (1952)

CAN'T BUY ME LOVE (Lennon–McCartney)
The Beatles in *A Hard Day's Night* (1964)

CAN'T HELP SINGING (Kern–Harburg)
Deanna Durbin and Robert Paige in *Can't Help Singing* (1945)

THE CARIOCA (Youmans–Kahn–Eliscu)
Etta Moten (danced by Fred Astaire and Ginger Rogers) in *Flying Down To Rio* (1933)

CAROLINA IN THE MORNING (Donaldson–Kahn)
Betty Grable and June Haver in *The Dolly Sisters* (1945)
Robert Alda and Ann Sothern in *April Showers* (1948)
Patrice Wymore in *I'll See You In My Dreams* (1951)

CHANGE PARTNERS (Berlin)
Fred Astaire to Ginger Rogers in *Carefree* (1938)

CHATTANOOGA CHOO-CHOO (Warren–Gordon)
Tex Beneke, The Modernaires and Glenn Miller And His Orchestra, plus Dorothy Dandridge and The

Nicholas Brothers in *Sun Valley Serenade* (1941)

Dan Dailey in *You're My Everything* (1949)

CHEEK TO CHEEK (Berlin)
Fred Astaire to Ginger Rogers in *Top Hat* (1935)

CHICA, CHICA, BOOM CHIC (Warren–Gordon)
Carmen Miranda in *That Night In Rio* (1941)

CHIM CHIM CHEREE (R. M. and R. B. Sherman)
Julie Andrews and Dick Van Dyke in *Mary Poppins* (1964)

CLIMB EV'RY MOUNTAIN (Rodgers–Hammerstein)
Peggy Wood in *The Sound Of Music* (1965)

COAL MINER'S DAUGHTER (Lynn)
Sissy Spacek as Loretta Lynn in *Coal Miner's Daughter* (1980)

COMEDY TONIGHT (Sondheim)
Zero Mostel in *A Funny Thing Happened On The Way To The Forum* (1966)

THE CONTINENTAL (Conrad–Magidson)
Ginger Rogers with Erik Rhodes and Lillian Miles in *The Gay Divorcee* (1934)

COUNT YOUR BLESSINGS (INSTEAD OF SHEEP) (Berlin)
Bing Crosby and Rosemary Clooney in *White Christmas* (1954)

A COUPLE OF SONG AND DANCE MEN (Berlin)
Bing Crosby and Fred Astaire in *Blue Skies* (1946)

A COUPLE OF SWELLS (Berlin)
Fred Astaire and Judy Garland in *Easter Parade* (1948)

COW-COW BOOGIE (Raye–DePaul–Carter)
Ella Mae Morse in *Reveille With Beverly* (1943)

CRY ME A RIVER (Hamilton)

Can't Help Singing (1945) was the last of the Deanna Durbin hits.

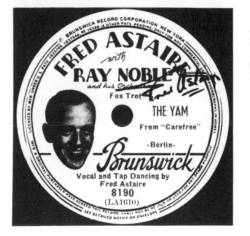

"The Yam" was an Astaire–Rogers dance number from 1938's *Carefree*, but was sung only by Ginger Rogers in the film.

Julie London in *The Girl Can't Help It* (1956)

CRYING FOR THE CAROLINES (Warren–Lewis–Young)
The Brox Sisters in *Spring Is Here* (1930)

CUANTO LE GUSTA (Gilbert–Ruiz)
Carmen Miranda in *A Date With Judy* (1948)

One of the first big-budget rock 'n' roll musicals, *The Girl Can't Help It* (1956), included Julie London singing her big hit, "Cry Me A River". She is seen here with Edmond O'Brien in a scene from the film.

DAMES (Warren–Dubin)
> Dick Powell and the Busby Berkeley chorines in *Dames* (1934)

DARK EYES (traditional)
> Al Jolson in *Wonder Bar* (1934)
> Raymond Paige And His Orchestra and Chorus in *Hollywood Hotel* (1937)
> (See "Otchi Tchorniya" in "Singers And Songs In Non-Musicals.")

DAY BY DAY (Schwartz)
> Robin Lamont in *Godspell* (1973)

DEARLY BELOVED (Kern–Mercer)
> Fred Astaire with Xavier Cugat And His Orchestra in *You Were Never Lovelier* (1942)

DIAMONDS ARE A GIRL'S BEST FRIEND (Styne–Robin)
> Marilyn Monroe in *Gentlemen Prefer Blondes* (1953)

DING-DONG, THE WITCH IS DEAD (Arlen–Harburg)
> Judy Garland And The Munchkins in *The Wizard Of Oz* (1939)

DO I LOVE YOU (Porter)
> Dick Haymes, The Pied Pipers, Gene Kelly and Tommy Dorsey And His Orchestra in *Dubarry Was A Lady* (1943)
> Ginny Simms in *Night And Day* (1946)

DOIN' WHAT COMES NATURALLY (Berlin)
> Betty Hutton in *Annie Get Your Gun* (1950)

THE DONKEY SERENADE (Friml–Stothart–Forrest–Wright)
> Allan Jones in *The Firefly* (1937)

DON'T FENCE ME IN (Porter)
> The Andrews Sisters, Roy Rogers and The Sons Of The Pioneers in *Hollywood Canteen* (1944)

DON'T GIVE UP THE SHIP (Warren–Dubin)

Dick Powell in *Shipmates Forever* (1935)

DON'T RAIN ON MY PARADE (Styne–Merrill)
Barbra Streisand in *Funny Girl* (1968)

DREAM LOVER (Schertzinger–Grey)
Jeanette MacDonald in *The Love Parade* (1929)

EASE ON DOWN THE ROAD (Smalls)
Diana Ross, Michael Jackson, Ted Ross and Nipsey Russell in *The Wiz* (1978)

EASTER PARADE (Berlin)
Don Ameche in *Alexander's Ragtime Band* (1938)
Bing Crosby in *Holiday Inn* (1942)
Judy Garland in *Easter Parade* (1948)

EASY TO LOVE (Porter)
James Stewart and Eleanor Powell in *Born To Dance* (1936)
Tony Martin in *Easy To Love* (1953)

EMBRACEABLE YOU (George and Ira Gershwin)
Dorothy Lee and Eddie Quillan in *Girl Crazy* (1932)
Judy Garland and Robert E. Strickland in *Girl Crazy* (1943)
Jane Froman for Susan Hayward as Jane Froman in *With A Song In My Heart* (1952)

EVERGREEN (Love Theme from A STAR IS BORN) (Streisand–Williams)
Barbra Streisand and Kris Kristofferson in *A Star Is Born* (1976)

EVERYTHING I HAVE IS YOURS (Lane–Adamson)
Art Jarrett and Joan Crawford in *Dancing Lady* (1933)
Monica Lewis in *Everything I Have Is Yours* (1952)

EVERYTHING'S COMING UP ROSES (Styne–Sondheim)
Rosalind Russell in *Gypsy* (1962)

FALLING IN LOVE WITH LOVE (Rodgers–Hart)
Allan Jones and Rosemary Lane in *The Boys From Syracuse* (1940)

FAME (Gore–Pitchford)
Irene Cara in *Fame* (1980)

FASCINATING RHYTHM (George and Ira Gershwin)
Eleanor Powell in *Lady Be Good* (1943)

The famous duo, Ginger Rogers and Fred Astaire sing "A Fine Romance" in *Swing Time* (1936).

Ginger Rogers and Fred Astaire stole the show in *Flying Down To Rio* (1933).

Tommy Dorsey And His Orchestra in *Girl Crazy* (1943)

A FELLA WITH AN UMBRELLA (Berlin)
Peter Lawford and Judy Garland in *Easter Parade* (1948)

A FINE ROMANCE (Kern–Fields)
Fred Astaire and Ginger Rogers in *Swing Time* (1936)

Virginia O'Brien in *Till The Clouds Roll By* (1946)

FIT AS A FIDDLE (Goodhart–Freed–Hoffman)
Gene Kelly and Donald O'Connor in *Singin' In The Rain* (1952)

FLYING DOWN TO RIO (Youmans–Kahn–Eliscu)
Fred Astaire singing on the ground, with Ginger Rogers and chorines flying overhead, in *Flying Down To Rio* (1933)

A FOGGY DAY (IN LONDON TOWN) (George and Ira Gershwin)
Fred Astaire in *A Damsel In Distress* (1937)

THE FOLKS WHO LIVE ON THE HILL (Kern–Hammerstein)
Irene Dunne in *High, Wide And Handsome* (1937)

FOR ME AND MY GAL (Meyer–Leslie–Goetz)
Gene Kelly and Judy Garland in *For Me And My Gal* (1942)

FORTY-SECOND STREET (Warren–Dubin)
Ruby Keeler and Dick Powell in *42nd Street* (1933)

FROM THIS MOMENT ON (Porter)
Ann Miller and Tommy Rall in *Kiss Me, Kate* (1953)

FUNNY FACE (George and Ira Gershwin)
Fred Astaire to Audrey Hepburn in *Funny Face* (1957)

A GAL IN CALICO (Schwartz–Robin)
Dennis Morgan, Jack Carson and Martha Vickers in *The Time, The Place And The Girl* (1946)

GET HAPPY (Arlen–Koehler)
Judy Garland in *Summer Stock* (UK: *If You Feel Like Singing*) (1950)

George Murphy, Judy Garland and Gene Kelly in *For Me And My Gal* (1942).

Jane Froman for Susan Hayward as Jane Froman in *With A Song In My Heart* (1952)

GETTING TO KNOW YOU (Rodgers–Hammerstein)
Marni Nixon for Deborah Kerr in *The King And I* (1956)

GIGI (Lerner–Loewe)
Louis Jourdan in *Gigi* (1958)

THE GIRL THAT I MARRY (Berlin)
Howard Keel in *Annie Get Your Gun* (1950)

GIVE ME THE SIMPLE LIFE (Bloom–Ruby)
John Payne and June Haver in *Wake Up And Dream* (1946)

GIVE MY REGARDS TO BROAD-WAY (Cohan)

Eddie Buzzel in *Little Johnnie Jones* (1929)

James Cagney as George M. Cohan in *Yankee Doodle Dandy* (1942)

Dan Dailey and Charles Winninger in *Give My Regards To Broadway* (1948)

Al Jolson for Larry Parks in *Jolson Sings Again* (1949)

Jane Froman for Susan Hayward as Jane Froman in *With A Song In My Heart* (1952)

GOD BLESS AMERICA (Berlin)

Kate Smith in *This Is The Army* (1943)

Jane Froman for Susan Hayward as Jane Froman in *With A Song In My Heart* (1952)

GOD BLESS THE CHILD (Herzog–Holiday)

Diana Ross as Billie Holiday in *Lady Sings The Blues* (1972)

GOING MY WAY (Van Heusen–Burke)

Bing Crosby in *Going My Way* (1944)

GOOD MORNING (Brown–Freed)

Judy Garland and Mickey Rooney in *Babes In Arms* (1939)

Gene Kelly, Debbie Reynolds and Donald O'Connor in *Singin' In The Rain* (1952)

GOODNIGHT, VIENNA (Posford–Maschwitz)

Jack Buchanan in *Goodnight, Vienna* (1932)

GREEN EYES (Utrera–Mendenez)

Jimmy Dorsey And His Orchestra with Helen O'Connell and Bob Eberly in *The Fabulous Dorseys* (1947)

HALLELUJAH (Youmans–Robin–Grey)

Tony Martin, Vic Damone and Russ Tamblyn in *Hit The Deck* (1955)

HAPPINESS IS JUST A THING CALLED JOE (Arlen–Harburg)

Ethel Waters in *Cabin In The Sky* (1943)

Susan Hayward in *I'll Cry Tomorrow* (1955)

HAPPY FEET (Ager–Yellen)

The Rhythm Boys (including Bing Crosby) and Paul Whiteman And His Orchestra in *King Of Jazz* (1930)

HAPPY HOLIDAY (Berlin)

Bing Crosby in *Holiday Inn* (1942)

HAPPY TALK (Rodgers–Hammerstein)

Muriel Smith for Juanita Hall in *South Pacific* (1958)

HAVE YOURSELF A MERRY LITTLE CHRISTMAS (Martin–Blane)

Judy Garland in *Meet Me In St. Louis* (1944)

HEAT WAVE (Berlin)

Olga San Juan in *Blue Skies* (1946)

Marilyn Monroe in *There's No Business Like Show Business* (1954)

HEIGH-HO, THE GANG'S ALL HERE (Adamson–Lane)

Fred Astaire and Joan Crawford in *Dancing Lady* (1933)

HELL HATH NO FURY (Brodszky–Cahn)

Frankie Laine in *Meet Me In Las Vegas* (UK: *Viva Las Vegas*) (1956)

HELLO DOLLY (Herman)

Barbra Streisand and Louis Armstrong in *Hello Dolly* (1969)

HELLO YOUNG LOVERS (Rodgers–Hammerstein)

Marni Nixon for Deborah Kerr in *The King And I* (1956)

HERNANDO'S HIDEAWAY (Adler–Ross)

Carol Haney in *The Pajama Game* (1957)

HEY THERE (Adler–Ross)

John Raitt and Doris Day in *The Pajama Game* (1957)

HI-LILI, HI-LO (Kaper–Deutsch)
Leslie Caron and Mel Ferrer in *Lili* (1953)

HIT THE ROAD TO DREAMLAND (Arlen–Mercer)
Dick Powell and Mary Martin with The Golden Gate Quartet in *Star Spangled Rhythm* (1942)

HONEYSUCKLE ROSE (Waller–Razaf)
Betty Grable in *Tin Pan Alley* (1940)
Lena Horne in *Thousands Cheer* (1943)
Diahnne Abbott in *New York, New York* (1977)

HONOLULU (Warren–Kahn)
Eleanor Powell and Gracie Allen in *Honolulu* (1939)

HOORAY FOR CAPTAIN SPAULD-ING (Kalmar–Ruby)
Groucho Marx, Margaret Dumont, Zeppo Marx and Robert Greig in *Animal Crackers* (1930)

HOORAY FOR HOLLYWOOD (Whiting–Mercer)
Benny Goodman And His Orchestra with Johnnie "Scat" Davis and Frances Langford in *Hollywood Hotel* (1937)
Sammy Cahn wrote an alternative lyric which Sammy Davis Jr. sang in *Pepe* (1961)

HOPELESSLY DEVOTED TO YOU (Farrar)
Olivia Newton-John in *Grease* (1978)

THE HOSTESS WITH THE MOSTES' ON THE BALL (Berlin)
Ethel Merman in *Call Me Madam* (1953)

HOW ABOUT YOU (Lane–Freed)
Judy Garland and Mickey Rooney in *Babes On Broadway* (1941)

HOW ARE THINGS IN GLOCCA

MORRA (Lane–Harburg)
Petula Clark in *Finian's Rainbow* (1968)

HOW COULD YOU BELIEVE ME WHEN I SAID I LOVED YOU (WHEN YOU KNOW I'VE BEEN A LIAR ALL MY LIFE) (Lane–Lerner)
Fred Astaire and Jane Powell in *Royal Wedding* (UK: *Wedding Bells*) (1951)

An original advertisement for *Hollywood Hotel* (1937). It was a film typical of the star-studded musicals of its day.

HOW DEEP IS THE OCEAN (Berlin)
Bing Crosby in *Blue Skies* (1946)
Frank Sinatra in *Meet Danny Wilson* (1952)

HOW LONG HAS THIS BEEN GOING ON (George and Ira Gershwin)
Audrey Hepburn in *Funny Face* (1957)

HOW LUCKY CAN YOU GET (Kander–Ebb)
Barbra Streisand in *Funny Lady* (1975)

HOW TO HANDLE A WOMAN (Lerner–Loewe)
Richard Harris in *Camelot* (1967)

A HUBBA-HUBBA-HUBBA (DIG YOU LATER) (Adamson–McHugh)
Perry Como in *Doll Face* (UK: *Come Back To Me*) (1945)

I CAN'T BEGIN TO TELL YOU (Monaco–Gordon)
Betty Grable and John Payne in *The Dolly Sisters* (1945)

I CAN'T GIVE YOU ANYTHING BUT LOVE, BABY (McHugh–Fields)
Judy Canova in *True To The Army* (1942)
Lena Horne and Bill Robinson in *Stormy Weather* (1943)
Gloria De Haven in *So This Is Paris* (1954)

I COULD HAVE DANCED ALL NIGHT (Lerner–Loewe)
Audrey Hepburn in *My Fair Lady* (1964)

I COULD WRITE A BOOK (Rodgers–Hart)
Frank Sinatra in *Pal Joey* (1957)

I COULDN'T SLEEP A WINK LAST NIGHT (McHugh–Adamson)
Frank Sinatra in *Higher And Higher* (1944)
Skinnay Ennis And His Orchestra in *Radio Stars On Parade* (1945)

I CRIED FOR YOU (Arnheim–Lyman–Freed)
Judy Garland in *Babes In Arms* (1939)
Helen Forrest with Harry James And His Music Makers in *Bathing Beauty* (1944)

I DON'T KNOW HOW TO LOVE HIM (Webber–Rice)
Yvonne Elliman in *Jesus Christ Superstar* (1973)

I DON'T WANT TO WALK WITHOUT YOU (Styne–Loesser)
Johnnie Johnston and Betty Jane Rhodes in *Sweater Girl* (1941)

I FALL TO PIECES (Cochran–Howard)
Beverly D'Angelo as Patsy Cline in *Coal Miner's Daughter* (1980)

I FEEL A SONG COMIN' ON (McHugh–Fields–Oppenheimer)
Frances Langford and Alice Faye in *Every Night At Eight* (1935)

I FOUND A MILLION DOLLAR BABY (IN A FIVE AND TEN CENT STORE) (Warren–Rose–Dixon)
Barbra Streisand in *Funny Lady* (1975)

I GET A KICK OUT OF YOU (Porter)
Ethel Merman and Bing Crosby in *Anything Goes* (1936)
Mitzi Gaynor and Bing Crosby in *Anything Goes* (1956)

I GOT RHYTHM (George and Ira Gershwin)
Kitty Kelly in *Girl Crazy* (1932)
Judy Garland with Tommy Dorsey And His Orchestra in *Girl Crazy* (1943)
Gene Kelly and a children's chorus in *An American In Paris* (1951)

I GUESS I'LL HAVE TO CHANGE MY PLANS (Schwartz–Dietz)
Fred Astaire and Jack Buchanan in *The Band Wagon* (1953)

I HAD THE CRAZIEST DREAM

(Warren–Gordon)
Helen Forrest with Harry James And His Music Makers in *Springtime In The Rockies* (1942)

I KNOW WHY (AND SO DO YOU) (Warren–Gordon)
Glenn Miller And His Orchestra with The Modernaires, and Pat Friday for Lynn Bari, in *Sun Valley Serenade* (1941)

I LOVE A PIANO (Berlin)
Fred Astaire and Judy Garland in *Easter Parade* (1948)

I LOVE PARIS (Porter)
Frank Sinatra in *Can-Can* (1960)

I MAY BE WRONG BUT I THINK YOU'RE WONDERFUL (Sullivan–Ruskin)
Doris Day in *Young Man With A Horn* (1950)
Jane Wyman in *Starlift* (1951)

I ONLY HAVE EYES FOR YOU (Warren–Dubin)
Dick Powell and Ruby Keeler in *Dames* (1934)
Gordon MacRae in *Tea For Two* (1950)

I REMEMBER IT WELL (Lerner–Loewe)
Maurice Chevalier and Hermione Gingold in *Gigi* (1958)

I REMEMBER YOU (Schertzinger–Mercer)
Dorothy Lamour in *The Fleet's In* (1942)

I USED TO BE COLOR BLIND (Berlin)
Fred Astaire to Ginger Rogers in *Carefree* (1938)

I WHISTLE A HAPPY TUNE (Rodgers–Hammerstein)
Marni Nixon for Deborah Kerr in *The King And I* (1956)

I WISH I KNEW (Warren–Gordon)
Dick Haymes and Betty Grable in *Billy Rose's Diamond Horseshoe* (1945)

I WISH I WERE IN LOVE AGAIN (Rodgers–Hart)
Mickey Rooney and Judy Garland in *Words And Music* (1948)

I WON'T DANCE (Kern–Hammerstein–Harbach)
Fred Astaire in *Roberta* (1935)
Van Johnson and Lucille Bremer in *Till The Clouds Roll By* (1946)

I YI, YI, YI, I LIKE YOU VERY MUCH (Warren–Gordon)
Carmen Miranda in *That Night In Rio* (1941)

Songwriters Harry Warren and Al Dubin at work in their Hollywood studio. They wrote for many musicals in the 1930s.

A 78 picture label for Carmen Miranda's studio recording of one of her featured songs from the 1941 musical *That Night In Rio*.

I'D RATHER BE BLUE OVER YOU (Fisher–Rose)
Fanny Brice in *My Man* (1928)
Barbra Streisand in *Funny Girl* (1968)

I'LL BUILD A STAIRWAY TO PARADISE (Gershwin–Goetz–DeSylva)
Georges Guetary in *An American In Paris* (1951)

I'LL GET BY (Alhert–Turk)
Dan Dailey in *You Were Meant For Me* (1948)

I'LL SEE YOU IN MY DREAMS (Jones–Kahn)
Doris Day in *I'll See You In My Dreams* (1951)

I'LL SING YOU A THOUSAND LOVE SONGS (Warren–Dubin)
Sung by Bob Page to Marion Davies in *Cain And Mabel* (1936)

I'LL STRING ALONG WITH YOU (Warren–Dubin)
Dick Powell and Ginger Rogers in *Twenty Million Sweethearts* (1934)
Jack Carson and Joan Leslie in *The Hard Way* (1942)
Doris Day in *My Dream Is Yours* (1949)

I'LL WALK ALONE (Styne–Cahn)
Dinah Shore in *Follow The Boys* (1944)
Jane Froman for Susan Hayward as Jane Froman in *With A Song In My Heart* (1952)

I'M ALWAYS CHASING RAINBOWS (Carroll–McCarthy)
Betty Grable and John Payne in *The Dolly Sisters* (1945)

I'M EASY (Carradine)
Keith Carradine in *Nashville* (1975)

I'M GETTIN' SENTIMENTAL OVER YOU (Bassman–Washington)
Tommy Dorsey And His Orchestra in *A Song Is Born* (1948)

I'M GONNA WASH THAT MAN RIGHT OUTA MY HAIR (Rodgers–Hammerstein)
Mitzi Gaynor in *South Pacific* (1958)

I'M IN THE MOOD FOR LOVE (McHugh–Fields)
Frances Langford in *Every Night At Eight* (1935)
Frances Langford in *Palm Springs* (1936)
Gloria DeHaven in *Between Two Women* (1944)

I'M JUST WILD ABOUT HARRY (Blake–Sissle)
Alice Faye in *Rose Of Washington Square* (1939)

I'M PUTTING ALL MY EGGS IN ONE BASKET (Berlin)

Fred Astaire and Ginger Rogers in *Follow The Fleet* (1936)

I'M SITTIN' ON TOP OF THE WORLD (Henderson–Lewis–Young)

Al Jolson in *The Singing Fool* (1928)

I'VE GOT A CRUSH ON YOU (George and Ira Gershwin)

Frank Sinatra in *Meet Danny Wilson* (1952)

I'VE GOT A FEELING FOR YOU (Trent–Alter)

Joan Crawford in *Hollywood Revue Of 1929* (1929)

I'VE GOT A FEELIN' YOU'RE FOOLIN' (Brown–Freed)

Robert Taylor, Eleanor Powell and June Knight in *Broadway Melody Of 1936* (1935)

Jane Froman for Susan Hayward as Jane Froman in *With A Song In My Heart* (1952)

I'VE GOT A GAL IN KALAMAZOO

(Warren–Gordon)

Tex Beneke, Marion Hutton, The Modernaires and Glenn Miller And His Orchestra in *Orchestra Wives* (1942)

I'VE GOT MY LOVE TO KEEP ME WARM (Berlin)

Alice Faye and Dick Powell in *On The Avenue* (1937)

I'VE GOT THE WORLD ON A STRING (Arlen–Koehler)

Gloria DeHaven and June Haver in *I'll Get By* (1950)

I'VE GOT YOU UNDER MY SKIN (Porter)

Virginia Bruce in *Born To Dance* (1936)

Ginny Simms in *Night And Day* (1946)

Above: Elegant French singer Georges Guetary is surrounded by a bevy of Metro beauties on the set of his memorable "I'll Build A Stairway to Paradise" in *An Amerian In Paris* (1951).

Left: "I'll Sing You A Thousand Love Songs" was sung by Bob Page to Mavion Davies in *Cain and Mabel* (1936).

The highly successful *State Fair* (1945) made a star of Jeanne Crain, though her songs were dubbed for her by Louanne Hogan.

I'VE TOLD EV'RY LITTLE STAR (Kern–Hammerstein)
Gloria Swanson in *Music In The Air* (1934)

IF HE WALKED INTO MY LIFE (Herman)
Lucille Ball in *Mame* (1974)

IF I HAD A TALKING PICTURE OF YOU (DeSylva–Brown–Henderson)
Janet Gaynor and Charles Farrell in *Sunny Side Up* (1929)

IF I HAD MY WAY (Kendis–Klein)
Bing Crosby in *If I Had My Way* (1940)
Gale Storm and Phil Regan in *Sunbonnet Sue* (1946)

IF I HAD YOU (Shapiro–Campbell–Connelly)
Dan Dailey in *You Were Meant For Me* (1948)

IF I LOVED YOU (Rodgers–Hammerstein)
Gordon MacRae and Shirley Jones in *Carousel* (1956)

IF I ONLY HAD A BRAIN (Arlen–Harburg)
Ray Bolger, Bert Lahr and Jack Haley in *The Wizard Of Oz* (1939)

IF I WERE A RICH MAN (Bock–Harnick)
Topol in *Fiddler On The Roof* (1971)

IF MY FRIENDS COULD SEE ME NOW (Coleman–Fields)
Shirley MacLaine in *Sweet Charity* (1968)

IF YOU FEEL LIKE SINGING, SING (Warren–Gordon)
Judy Garland in *Summer Stock* (UK: *If You Feel Like Singing*) (1950)

THE IMPOSSIBLE DREAM (Leigh–Darion)
Peter O'Toole in *Man Of La Mancha* (1972)

IN LOVE IN VAIN (Kern–Robin)
Louanne Hogan for Jeanne Crain in *Centennial Summer* (1946)

IN THE COOL, COOL, COOL OF THE EVENING (Carmichael–Mercer)
Bing Crosby and Jane Wyman in *Here Comes The Groom* (1951)

IN THE MOOD (Garland–Razaf)
Glenn Miller And His Orchestra in *Sun Valley Serenade* (1941)

IN THE STILL OF THE NIGHT (Porter)
Nelson Eddy in *Rosalie* (1937)

INDIAN LOVE CALL (Friml–Hammerstein–Harbach)
Jeanette MacDonald and Nelson Eddy in *Rose Marie* (1936)
Howard Keel and Ann Blyth in *Rose Marie* (1954)

ISN'T IT ROMANTIC (Rodgers–Hart)
Jeanette MacDonald and Maurice Chevalier in *Love Me Tonight* (1932)

ISN'T THIS A LOVELY DAY TO BE

CAUGHT IN THE RAIN (Berlin)
Fred Astaire to Ginger Rogers in *Top Hat* (1935)

IT COULD HAPPEN TO YOU (Burke–Van Heusen)
Fred MacMurray and Dorothy Lamour in *And The Angels Sing* (1944)

IT HAD TO BE YOU (Jones–Kahn)
Eddie Cantor in *Show Business* (1944)
Danny Thomas in *I'll See You In My Dreams* (1951)

IT HAPPENED IN MONTEREY (Wayne–Rose)
John Boles with Paul Whiteman And His Orchestra in *King Of Jazz* (1930)

IT MIGHT AS WELL BE SPRING (Rodgers–Hammerstein)
Louanne Hogan for Jeanne Crain in *State Fair* (1945)

IT'S A GRAND NIGHT FOR SING-ING (Rodgers–Hammerstein)
Dick Haymes in *State Fair* (1945)

IT'S A LOVELY DAY TODAY (Berlin)
Vera-Ellen and Donald O'Connor in *Call Me Madam* (1953)

IT'S A MOST UNUSUAL DAY (McHugh–Adamson)
Jane Powell in *A Date With Judy* (1948)

IT'S ALRIGHT WITH ME (Porter)
Frank Sinatra in *Can-Can* (1960)

IT'S EASY TO REMEMBER (Rodgers–Hart)
Bing Crosby in *Mississippi* (1935)

IT'S MAGIC (Styne–Cahn)
Doris Day in *Romance On The High Seas* (UK: *It's Magic*) (1948)

JAILHOUSE ROCK (Leiber–Stoller)
Elvis Presley in *Jailhouse Rock* (1957)

LE JAZZ HOT (Mancini–Bricusse)
Julie Andrews in *Victor, Victoria* (1982)

JEEPERS CREEPERS (Warren–Mercer)
Louis Armstrong in *Going Places* (1938). Briefly, by Joyce Reynolds and Charles Smith, in *Yankee Doodle Dandy* (1942)

JOHN HENRY (Handy)
Paul Robeson and The Hall Johnson Choir in *Emperor Jones* (1933)

JOHNNY ONE NOTE (Rodgers–Hart)
Judy Garland in *Words And Music* (1948)

JUNE IN JANUARY (Rainger–Robin)
Bing Crosby in *Here Is My Heart* (1934)

JUNE IS BUSTIN' OUT ALL OVER (Rodgers–Hammerstein)
Barbara Ruick and Claramae Turner in *Carousel* (1956)

Louis Armstrong and Maxine Sullivan in *Going Places* (1938).

JUST IN TIME (Styne–Comden–Green)
Judy Holliday and Dean Martin in *Bells Are Ringing* (1960)

JUST ONE OF THOSE THINGS (Porter)
Ginny Simms in *Night And Day* (1945)
Doris Day in *Lullaby Of Broadway* (1951)
Peggy Lee in *The Jazz Singer* (1953)
Frank Sinatra in *Young At Heart* (1955)
Maurice Chevalier in *Can-Can* (1960)
Burt Reynolds in *At Long Last Love* (1975)

KEEP YOUNG AND BEAUTIFUL (Warren–Dubin)
Eddie Cantor in *Roman Scandals* (1933)

KISS THE BOYS GOODBYE (Schertzinger–Loesser)
Mary Martin in *Kiss The Boys Goodbye* (1941)

KOL NIDRE (Traditional)
Al Jolson in *The Jazz Singer* (1927)
Danny Thomas in *The Jazz Singer* (1952)
Neil Diamond in *The Jazz Singer* (1980)

THE LADY IN THE TUTTI-FRUTTI HAT (Warren–Gordon)
Carmen Miranda in *The Gang's All Here* (UK: *The Girls He Left Behind*) (1943)

THE LADY IS A TRAMP (Rodgers–Hart)
Judy Garland in *Babes In Arms* (1939)
Lena Horne in *Words And Music* (1948)
Frank Sinatra in *Pal Joey* (1957)

LAST DANCE (Jabara)
Donna Summer in *Thank God It's Friday* (1978)

THE LAST TIME I SAW PARIS (Kern–Hammerstein)
Dinah Shore in *Till The Clouds Roll By* (1946)

LAZY (Berlin)
Bing Crosby in *Holiday Inn* (1942)
Marilyn Monroe in *There's No Business Like Show . Business* (1954)

LET ME SING AND I'M HAPPY (Berlin)
Al Jolson in *Mammy* (1930)
Al Jolson on the soundtrack of *The Jolson Story* (1946)

LET THE REST OF THE WORLD GO BY (Ball–Brennan)
Dick Haymes in *When Irish Eyes Are Smiling* (1944)

LET YOURSELF GO (Berlin)
Ginger Rogers in *Follow The Fleet* (1936)

LET'S CALL THE WHOLE THING OFF (George and Ira Gershwin)
Fred Astaire and Ginger Rogers in *Shall We Dance* (1937)

LET'S FACE THE MUSIC AND DANCE (Berlin)
Fred Astaire to Ginger Rogers in *Follow The Fleet* (1936)
(This original sequence was used in the 1981 film *Pennies From Heaven*.)

LET'S K-NOCK K-NEES (Gordon–Revel)
Betty Grable and Edward Everett Horton in *The Gay Divorcee* (1934)

LET'S START THE NEW YEAR RIGHT (Berlin)
Bing Crosby in *Holiday Inn* (1942)

A LITTLE GIRL FROM LITTLE ROCK (Styne–Robin)
Marilyn Monroe and Jane Russell in *Gentlemen Prefer Blondes* (1953)

Frank Sinatra sings "A Lovely Way To Spend An Evening" to Michele Morgan, with Dooley Wilson on the piano, in *Higher And Higher* (1944).

THE LITTLE THINGS YOU USED TO DO (Warren–Dubin)
Helen Morgan in *Go Into Your Dance* (1935)

LONG AGO AND FAR AWAY (Kern–Gershwin)
Gene Kelly and Martha Mears for Rita Hayworth in *Cover Girl* (1944)
Kathryn Grayson in *Till The Clouds Roll By* (1946)

LOOK FOR THE SILVER LINING (Kern–DeSylva)
Marilyn Miller in *Sally* (1929)
Judy Garland in *Till The Clouds Roll By* (1946)
June Haver in *Look For The Silver Lining* (1949)

LOUISE (Whiting–Robin)
Maurice Chevalier in *Innocents Of Paris* (1929)

LOVE (Blane–Martin)
Lena Horne in *Ziegfeld Follies* (1946)

LOVE IN BLOOM (Rainger–Robin)
Bing Crosby in *She Loves Me Not* (1935)
Judy Canova in *True To The Army* (1942)

LOVE IS HERE TO STAY (George and Ira Gershwin)
Kenny Baker in *The Goldwyn Follies* (1938)
Gene Kelly in *An American In Paris* (1951)

LOVE IS JUST AROUND THE

117

CORNER (Robin–Gensler)
Bing Crosby in *Here Is My Heart* (1934)

LOVE ISN'T BORN, IT'S MADE (Schwartz–Loesser)
Ann Sheridan in *Thank Your Lucky Stars* (1943)

LOVE ME OR LEAVE ME (Donaldson–Kahn)
Patrice Wymore in *I'll See You In My Dreams* (1951)
Doris Day in *Love Me Or Leave Me* (1955)

LOVE ON THE ROCKS (Diamond–Becaud)
Neil Diamond in *The Jazz Singer* (1980)

LOVE THY NEIGHBOR (Gordon–Revel)
Bing Crosby in *We're Not Dressing* (1934)

THE LOVELIEST NIGHT OF THE YEAR (Aaronson–Webster)
Ann Blyth in *The Great Caruso* (1951)

LOVELY LADY (McHugh–Koehler)
Kenny Baker in *King Of Burlesque* (1935)

A LOVELY WAY TO SPEND AN EVENING (McHugh–Adamson)
Frank Sinatra in *Higher And Higher* (1944)

LOVER (Rodgers–Hart)
Jeanette MacDonald in *Love Me Tonight* (1932)
Deanna Durbin in *Because Of Him* (1946)
Peggy Lee in *The Jazz Singer* (1953)

LOVER COME BACK TO ME (Romberg–Hammerstein)
Grace Moore in *New Moon* (1930)
Jeanette MacDonald in *New Moon* (1940)
Tony Martin in *Deep In My Heart* (1954)

LUCK BE A LADY TONIGHT (Loesser)
Marlon Brando in *Guys And Dolls* (1955)

LUCKY IN LOVE (DeSylva–Brown–Henderson)
Mel Torme, Peter Lawford and June Allyson in *Good News* (1947)

LULLABY OF BROADWAY (Warren–Dubin)
Winifred Shaw and Dick Powell in *Gold Diggers Of 1935* (1935)
Doris Day in *Lullaby Of Broadway* (1951)

LULU'S BACK IN TOWN (Warren–Dubin)
Dick Powell and The Mills Brothers in *Broadway Gondolier* (1935)

MA, HE'S MAKING EYES AT ME (Conrad–Clare)
Judy Canova in *Singin' In The Corn* (1946)

MAKE BELIEVE (Kern–Hammerstein)
Irene Dunne and Allan Jones in *Showboat* (1936)
Kathryn Grayson and Tony Martin in *Till The Clouds Roll By* (1945)
Kathryn Grayson and Howard Keel in *Showboat* (1951)

MAKIN' WHOOPEE (Donaldson–Kahn)
Eddie Cantor in *Whoopee* (1930)
Eddie Cantor in *Show Business* (1944)
Doris Day and Danny Thomas in *I'll See You In My Dreams* (1951)
Eddie Cantor for Keefe Brasselle as Eddie Cantor in *The Eddie Cantor Story* (1953)

MAME (Herman)
Robert Preston in *Mame* (1974)

THE MAN I LOVE (George and Ira Gershwin)

Marlon Brando sings "Luck Be A Lady Tonight" in the film version of Damon Runyon's *Guys And Dolls* (1955).

Hazel Scott in *Rhapsody In Blue* (1945)

Gogi Grant for Ann Blyth as Helen Morgan in *The Helen Morgan Story* (UK: *Both Ends Of The Candle*) (1957)

Diana Ross in *Lady Sings The Blues* (1972)

Liza Minnelli in *New York, New York* (1977)

THE MAN THAT GOT AWAY (Arlen–Gershwin)
Judy Garland in *A Star Is Born* (1954)

MANHATTAN (Rodgers–Hart)
Mickey Rooney in *Words And Music* (1948)

Played by Carmen Cavallaro for Tyrone Power as Eddy Duchin in *The Eddy Duchin Story* (1956)
Bob Hope and Vera Miles in *Beau James* (1957)

MARIA (Bernstein–Sondheim)
Jim Bryant for Richard Beymer in *West Side Story* (1961)

MAYBE THIS TIME (Kander–Ebb)
Liza Minnelli in *Cabaret* (1972)

MEET ME IN ST. LOUIS (Sterling–Mills)
Judy Garland and Lucille Bremer in *Meet Me In St. Louis* (1944)

MIMI (Rodgers–Hart)
Maurice Chevalier in *Love Me Tonight* (1932)

119

MINNIE FROM TRINIDAD (Edens)
Judy Garland in *Ziegfeld Girl* (1941)

MINNIE THE MOOCHER (Calloway–Mills)
Cab Calloway in *The Big Broadcast* (1932)
Cab Calloway in *The Blues Brothers* (1980)

MISS OTIS REGRETS (Porter)
Monty Woolley in *Night And Day* (1946)

MISSISSIPPI MUD (Cavanaugh–Barris)
The Rhythm Boys (including Bing Crosby) in *King Of Jazz* (1930)

MISTER GALLAGHER AND MISTER SHEAN (Gallagher–Shean)
Al Shean and Charles Winninger as Pop Gallagher in *Ziegfeld Girl* (1941)
Jack Benny and Al Shean in *Atlantic City* (1944)

MOONLIGHT AND ROSES (Black–Moret–Lemare)
Betty Grable in *Tin Pan Alley* (1940)

MOONLIGHT BAY (Madden–Wenrich)
Alice Faye in *Tin Pan Alley* (1940)
Doris Day in *On Moonlight Bay* (1951)

MOONLIGHT BECOMES YOU (Burke–Van Heusen)
Bing Crosby to Dorothy Lamour in *Road To Morocco* (1942)

MOONLIGHT SERENADE (Miller–Parish)
Glenn Miller And His Orchestra in *Orchestra Wives* (1942)

MORE AND MORE (Kern–Harburg)
Deanna Durbin in *Can't Help Singing* (1944)

THE MORE I SEE YOU (Warren–Gordon)
Dick Haymes to Betty Grable in *Billy Rose's Diamond Horseshoe* (1945)

MORE THAN YOU KNOW (Rose–Eliscu–Youmans)
Tony Martin in *Hit The Deck* (1955)
Barbra Streisand as Fanny Brice in *Funny Lady* (1975)

MY BABY JUST CARES FOR ME (Donaldson–Kahn)
Eddie Cantor in *Whoopee* (1930)

MY BLUE HEAVEN (Donaldson–Whiting)
Frances Langford in *Never A Dull Moment* (1943)
Betty Grable and Dan Dailey in *My Blue Heaven* (1949)

MY BUDDY (Donaldson–Kahn)
Doris Day in *I'll See You In My Dreams* (1952)

MY DREAM IS YOURS (Warren–Freed)
Doris Day in *My Dream Is Yours* (1949)

MY FUNNY VALENTINE (Rodgers–Hart)
Trudy Erwin for Kim Novak in *Pal Joey* (1957)

MY HEART BELONGS TO DADDY (Porter)
Mary Martin in *Love Thy Neighbor* (1940)
Mary Martin in *Night And Day* (1945)
Marilyn Monroe in *Let's Make Love* (1960)

MY IDEAL (Whiting–Robin)
Maurice Chevalier in *Playboy Of Paris* (1930)

MY KIND OF TOWN (Van Heusen–Cahn)
Frank Sinatra in *Robin And The Seven Hoods* (1964)

MY MAMMY (Donaldson–Young)
Al Jolson in *The Jazz Singer* (1927)
Al Jolson in *Rose Of Washington Square* (1939)
Al Jolson for Larry Parks as Al Jolson in *The Jolson Story* (1946)

MY MAN (Yvain–Pollock)

Fanny Brice in *My Man* (1929)
Alice Faye in *Rose Of Washington Square* (1939)
Barbra Streisand as Fanny Brice in *Funny Girl* (1968)
Diana Ross as Billie Holiday in *Lady Sings The Blues* (1972)
MY MELANCHOLY BABY (Burnett–Norton)
Bing Crosby in *Birth Of The Blues* (1941)
Benny Fields in *Minstrel Man* (1944)
Judy Garland in *A Star Is Born* (1954)
MY WILD IRISH ROSE (Olcott)
Dennis Morgan in *My Wild Irish Rose* (1947)

THE NEARNESS OF YOU (Carmichael–Washington)
Gladys Swarthout in *Romance In The Dark* (1938)
NEVER GONNA DANCE (Kern–Fields)
Fred Astaire to Ginger Rogers in *Swing Time* (1936)
NEVER IN A MILLION YEARS (Gordon–Revel)
Alice Faye and Jack Haley in *Wake Up And Live* (1937)
NEW YORK, NEW YORK (Bernstein–Comden–Green)
Frank Sinatra, Gene Kelly and Jules Munshin, as the sailors on a 24-hour shore leave, in *On The Town* (1949)
(not to be confused with "Theme From New York, New York", listed under that exact title)
NICE WORK IF YOU CAN GET IT (George and Ira Gershwin)
Fred Astaire in *A Damsel In Distress* (1937)
Georges Guetary in *An American In Paris* (1951)
NIGHT AND DAY (Porter)

Marilyn Monroe sang "My Heart Belongs To Daddy" in *Let's Make Love* (1960). It was also sung by Mary Martin in *Love Thy Neighbour* (1940) and *Night And Day* (1946).

Fred Astaire in *The Gay Divorcee* (1934)
Frank Sinatra in *Reveille With Beverly* (1943)
Cary Grant (as Porter) with Alexis Smith in *Night And Day* (1946)
THE NIGHT THEY INVENTED CHAMPAGNE (Lerner–Loewe)
Leslie Caron, Louis Jourdan and Hermione Gingold in *Gigi* (1959)
THE NIGHT WAS MADE FOR LOVE (Kern–Harbach)
Ramon Novarro in *The Cat And The Fiddle* (1934)
NO LOVE, NO NOTHIN' (Warren–Robin)
Alice Faye in *The Gang's All Here* (1943)
NO STRINGS (Berlin)
Fred Astaire in *Top Hat* (1935)

OH, HOW I HATE TO GET UP IN THE MORNING (Berlin)
Jack Haley in *Alexander's Ragtime Band* (1938)

121

Gordon MacRae as the Oklahoma cowboy in the screen version of the Rodgers and Hammerstein musical, *Oklahoma!* (1955).

Irving Berlin in *This Is The Army* (1943)

OH, WHAT A BEAUTIFUL MORNIN' (Rodgers–Hammerstein)
Gordon MacRae in *Oklahoma* (1955)

OH, YOU NASTY MAN (Henderson–Caesar–Yellen)
Alice Faye in *George White's Scandals* (1934)

OL' MAN RIVER (Hammerstein–Kern)
Paul Robeson in *Showboat* (1936)

Frank Sinatra in *Till The Clouds Roll By* (1946)
William Warfield in *Showboat* (1951)

ON THE ATCHISON, TOPEKA AND THE SANTA FE (Warren–Mercer)
Judy Garland in *The Harvey Girls* (1946)

ON THE STREET WHERE YOU LIVE (Lerner–Loewe)
Jeremy Brett in *My Fair Lady* (1964)

ON THE SUNNY SIDE OF THE STREET (Fields–McHugh)
Frankie Laine in *Sunny Side Of The Street* (1951)
Played by Carmen Cavallaro for Tyrone Power acting the part of Eddy Duchin in *The Eddy Duchin Story* (1956)

ONCE IN LOVE WITH AMY (Loesser)
Ray Bolger in *Where's Charley* (1952)

ONE ALONE (Romberg–Harbach–Hammerstein)
John Boles in *The Desert Song* (1929)
Dennis Morgan in *The Desert Song* (1943)

ONE FOR MY BABY (AND ONE MORE FOR THE ROAD) (Arlen–Mercer)
Fred Astaire in *The Sky's The Limit* (1943)
Frank Sinatra in *Young At Heart* (1955)

ONE HOUR WITH YOU (Whiting–Robin)
Maurice Chevalier and Jeanette MacDonald in *One Hour With You* (1932)

ONE NIGHT OF LOVE (Schertzinger–Kahn)
Grace Moore in *One Night Of Love* (1934)

ONLY A ROSE (Friml–Hooker)
Dennis King and Jeanette Mac-

Donald in *The Vagabond King* (1930)

Oreste in *The Vagabond King* (1956)

OUT HERE ON MY OWN (Gore–Pitchford)

Irene Cara in *Fame* (1980)

OVER MY SHOULDER (Woods)

Jessie Matthews in *Evergreen* (1934)

OVER THE RAINBOW (Arlen–Harburg)

Judy Garland in *The Wizard Of Oz* (1939)

OVER THERE (Cohan)

Frances Langford in *Yankee Doodle Dandy* (1942)

PAGAN LOVE SONG (Freed–Brown)

Ramon Novarro in *The Pagan* (1929)

Howard Keel in *Pagan Love Song* (1950)

PAINTING THE CLOUDS WITH SUNSHINE (Dubin–Burke)

Nick Lucas in *Gold Diggers Of Broadway* (1929)

Dennis Morgan and Lucille Norman in *Painting The Clouds With Sunshine* (1951)

THE PARTY'S OVER (Styne–Comden–Green)

Judy Holliday in *Bells Are Ringing* (1960)

PENNIES FROM HEAVEN (Johnston–Burke)

Bing Crosby to Edith Fellows in *Pennies From Heaven* (1936)

Dick Haymes in *Cruisin' Down The River* (1953)

Arthur Tracy's original recording for Vernel Barneris and Steve Martin in *Pennies From Heaven* (1981)

PEOPLE (Styne–Merrill)

Barbra Streisand in *Funny Girl* (1968)

PEOPLE LIKE YOU AND ME

(Warren–Gordon)

Tex Beneke, Marion Hutton, The Modernaires and Glenn Miller And His Orchestra in *Orchestra Wives* (1942)

PEOPLE WILL SAY WE'RE IN LOVE (Rodgers–Hammerstein)

Gordon MacRae and Shirley Jones in *Oklahoma* (1955)

PERSONALITY (Burke–Van Heusen)

Dorothy Lamour in *Road To Utopia* (1945)

THE PICCOLINO (Berlin)

Ginger Rogers in *Top Hat* (1935)

PICK YOURSELF UP (Kern–Fields)

Fred Astaire and Ginger Rogers in *Swing Time* (1936)

PINBALL WIZARD (Townshend)

Elton John in *Tommy* (1975)

PLAY A SIMPLE MELODY (Berlin)

Ethel Merman and Dan Dailey in *There's No Business Like Show Business* (1954)

PLEASE (Rainger–Robin)

Bing Crosby in *The Big Broadcast* (1932)

PRETTY BABY (Alstyne–Jackson–Kahn)

Al Jolson for Larry Parks as Al Jolson in *Jolson Sings Again* (1949)

Doris Day with Danny Thomas as Gus Kahn in *I'll See You In My Dreams* (1951)

A PRETTY GIRL IS LIKE A MELODY (Berlin)

Allan Jones for Dennis Morgan in *The Great Ziegfeld* (1936)

Ethel Merman in *Alexander's Ragtime Band* (1938)

Ethel Merman and Dan Dailey in *There's No Business Like Show Business* (1954)

PUT YOUR ARMS AROUND ME HONEY (Tilzer–McCree)

Judy Garland in *In The Good Old Summertime* (1949)

PUTTIN' ON THE RITZ (Berlin)

123

Irving Berlin and Ginger Rogers on the set of *Top Hat* (1935).

Harry Richman in *Puttin' On The Ritz* (1930)

Fred Astaire in *Blue Skies* (1946)

RAGTIME COWBOY JOE (Abrahams–Muir–Clarke)

Alice Faye in *Hello, Frisco, Hello* (1943)

Betty Hutton in *Incendiary Blonde* (1945)

THE RAINBOW CONNECTION (Williams–Ascher)

Jim Henson for Kermit, the frog, in *The Muppet Movie* (1979)

REMEMBER ME (Warren–Dubin)

Kenny Baker in *Mr Dodd Takes The Air* (1937)

REMEMBER MY FORGOTTEN MAN (Warren–Dubin)

Joan Blondell and Etta Moten in *Gold Diggers Of 1933* (1933)

RHAPSODY IN BLUE (George and Ira Gershwin)

Paul Whiteman And His Orchestra in *King Of Jazz* (1930)

Paul Whiteman And His Orchestra in *Rhapsody In Blue* (1945)

RHYTHM OF LIFE (Coleman–Fields)

Sammy Davis Jr. in *Sweet Charity* (1968)

RHYTHM OF THE RAIN (Meskill–Stern)

Maurice Chevalier and Ann Sothern in *Folies Bergères* (1935)

ROAD TO MOROCCO (Van Heusen–Burke)

Bing Crosby and Bob Hope riding a camel in *Road To Morocco* (1942)

(We're Gonna) ROCK AROUND THE CLOCK (Freedman–

DeKnight)
Bill Haley And His Comets in *Rock Around The Clock* (1956)

ROCK-A-BYE YOUR BABY WITH A DIXIE MELODY (Schwartz–Young–Lewis)
Sid Silvers in *Show Of Shows* (1929)
Al Jolson in *Rose Of Washington Square* (1939)
Al Jolson for Larry Parks as Al Jolson in *The Jolson Story* (1946)

THE ROSE (McBroom)
Bette Midler in *The Rose* (1979)

THE ROSE IN HER HAIR (Warren–Dubin)
Dick Powell (sung in English and Italian) in *Broadway Gondolier* (1935)
Chorus in a production medley serenading Marion Davies in *Cain And Mabel* (1936)

ROSE MARIE (Friml–Harbach–Hammerstein)
Nelson Eddy to Jeanette MacDonald in *Rose Marie* (1936)
Howard Keel to Ann Blyth in *Rose Marie* (1954)

ROSE OF WASHINGTON SQUARE (MacDonald–Hanley)
Alice Faye in *Rose Of Washington Square* (1939)

ST. LOUIS BLUES (Handy)
Bing Crosby in *Birth Of The Blues* (1941)
Nat "King" Cole and Eartha Kitt in *St. Louis Blues* (1958)

SAN FRANCISCO (Kaper–Kahn)
Jeanette MacDonald in *San Francisco* (1936)

SAND IN MY SHOES (Schertzinger–Loesser)
Connie Boswell in *Kiss The Boys Goodbye* (1941)

SECOND HAND ROSE (Hanley–Clarke)

Hollywood's favourite musical duo, Nelson Eddy and Jeanette MacDonald in *Rose Marie* (1936).

Fanny Brice in *My Man* (1928)
Barbra Streisand as Fanny Brice in *Funny Girl* (1968)

THE SECOND TIME AROUND (Van Heusen–Cahn)
Bing Crosby in *High Time* (1960)

SECRET LOVE (Fain–Webster)
Doris Day in *Calamity Jane* (1954)

SEPTEMBER IN THE RAIN (Warren–Dubin)
James Melton in *Melody For Two* (1937)

SEPTEMBER SONG (Weill–Anderson)
Charles Coburn in *Knickerbocker Holiday* (1944)

SERENADE (Romberg–Donnelly)
Mario Lanza for Edmund Purdom in *The Student Prince* (1954)
William Olvis in *Deep In My Heart* (1954)

SERENADE IN BLUE (Warren–Gordon)
Pat Friday for Lynn Bari and Glenn Miller And His Orchestra in *Orchestra Wives* (1942)

Nat "King" Cole, Eartha Kitt and Cab Calloway in *St Louis Blues* (1958).

SGT. PEPPER'S LONELY HEARTS CLUB BAND (Lennon–McCartney)
Peter Frampton, The Bee Gees, Paul Nicholas plus all-star lineup in *Sgt. Pepper's Lonely Heart's Club Band* (1979)

SEVENTY-SIX TROMBONES (Willson)
Robert Preston and chorus in *The Music Man* (1962)

SHADOW WALTZ (Warren–Dubin)
Dick Powell and Ruby Keeler in *Gold Diggers Of 1933* (1933)
Bob Page to Marion Davies in *Cain And Mabel* (1936)

SHAKIN' THE BLUES AWAY (Berlin)
Ann Miller in *Easter Parade* (1948)

SHALL WE DANCE (Rodgers–Hammerstein)
Yul Brynner and Marni Nixon for Deborah Kerr in *The King And I* (1956)

SHANGHAI LIL (Warren–Dubin)
James Cagney and Ruby Keeler in *Footlight Parade* (1933)

THE SHEIK OF ARABY (Snyder–Wheeler–Smith)
Alice Faye and Betty Grable dancing with Billy Gilbert in *Tin Pan Alley* (1940)

SHE'S A LATIN FROM MANHATTAN (Warren–Dubin)
Al Jolson (with interruptions from Sam Hayes) in *Go Into Your Dance* (UK: *Casino De Paris*) (1935)
Jack Carson in *The Hard Way* (1942)
Al Jolson for Larry Parks as Al

The Busby Berkeley girls with neon-lit violins perform a dazzling "Shadow Waltz" in *Gold Diggers Of 1933* (1933).

Jolson in *The Jolson Story* (1946)
SHINE ON, HARVEST MOON
(Bayes–Norworth)
Louis Prima in *Rose Of Washington Square* (1939)
Dennis Morgan in *Shine On Harvest Moon* (1944)
A SHINE ON YOUR SHOES
(Schwartz–Dietz)

Fred Astaire in *The Band Wagon* (1953)
SHOO SHOO BABY (Moore)
Ella Mae Morse in *South Of Dixie* (1944)
SHUFFLE OFF TO BUFFALO (Warren–Dubin)
Ruby Keeler, Clarence Nordstrum, Ginger Rogers and Una

One of the greatest of all movie musicals, *Singin' In The Rain* (1952), was also a biting satire about Hollywood during the late 1920s.

Merkel in *42nd Street* (1933)

SING YOU SINNERS (Coslow–Harding)
Lillian Roth in *Honey* (1930)
Billy Daniels in *Cruisin' Down The River* (1953)
Susan Hayward as Lillian Roth in *I'll Cry Tomorrow* (1955)

SINGIN' IN THE RAIN (Brown–Freed)

Cliff Edwards, The Brox Sisters and The Rounders in *Hollywood Revue Of 1929* (1929)
Jimmy Durante in *Speak Easily* (1932)
Judy Garland in *Little Nellie Kelly* (1940)
Gene Kelly with Debbie Reynolds and Donald O'Connor in *Singin' In The Rain* (1952)

THE SLIPPER AND THE ROSE WALTZ (HE DANCED WITH ME/SHE DANCED WITH ME) (R. M. and R. B. Sherman)
Richard Chamberlain and Gemma Craven in *The Slipper And The Rose* (1977)

SMALL FRY (Carmichael–Mercer)
Bing Crosby, Fred MacMurray and Donald O'Connor in *Sing You Sinners* (1938)

SMOKE GETS IN YOUR EYES (Kern–Harbach)
Irene Dunne in *Roberta* (1934)
Kathryn Grayson in *Lovely To Look At* (1952)

SO IN LOVE (Porter)
Kathryn Grayson and Howard Keel in *Kiss Me Kate* (1953)

SOLILOQUY (Rodgers–Hammerstein)
Gordon MacRae in *Carousel* (1956)

SOME ENCHANTED EVENING (Rodgers–Hammerstein)
Giorgio Tozzi for Rossano Brazzi in *South Pacific* (1958)

SOME OF THESE DAYS (Brooks)
Lillian Roth in *Animal Crackers* (1930)
Sophie Tucker in *Broadway Melody Of 1938* (1937)
Sophie Tucker in *Follow The Boys* (1944)

SOMEBODY LOVES ME (Gershwin–DeSylva–MacDonald)
Lena Horne in *Broadway Rhythm* (1944)

Doris Day in *Lullaby Of Broadway* (1951)

Betty Hutton as Blossom Seeley in *Somebody Loves Me* (1952)

Peggy Lee to Jack Webb in *Pete Kelly's Blues* (1955)

SOMETHING'S GOTTA GIVE (Mercer)

Fred Astaire in *Daddy Long Legs* (1955)

THE SONG'S GOTTA COME FROM THE HEART (Styne–Cahn)

Frank Sinatra and Jimmy Durante in *It Happened In Brooklyn* (1947)

SONNY BOY (DeSylva–Brown–Henderson–Jolson)

Al Jolson to Davey Lee in *The Singing Fool* (1928)

THE SOUND OF MUSIC (Rodgers–Hammerstein)

Julie Andrews in *The Sound Of Music* (1965)

SPEAK LOW (Weill–Nash)

Above: Frank Sinatra and Jimmy Durante sing "The Song's Gotta Come From The Heart" in *It Happened In Brooklyn* (1947). Sinatra's piano playing in this film was dubbed by André Previn.

Left: Fred Mac-Murray, Bing Crosby and a young Donald O'Connor perform "Small Fry" in a scene from *Sing You Sinners* (1938).

129

Dick Haymes and Eileen Wilson dubbing for Ava Gardner in *One Touch Of Venus* (1948)

SPRING IS HERE (Rodgers–Hart)
Jeanette MacDonald and Nelson Eddy in *I Married An Angel* (1942)

SPRING, SPRING, SPRING (DePaul–Mercer)
Chorus (including Russ Tamblyn, Tommy Rall and Julie Newmar) in *Seven Brides For Seven Brothers* (1954)

SPRING WILL BE A LITTLE LATE THIS YEAR (Loesser)
Deanna Durbin in *Christmas Holiday* (1944)

THE STANLEY STEAMER (Warren–Blane)
Mickey Rooney and Gloria De Haven in *Summer Holiday* (1946)

STAY AS SWEET AS YOU ARE (Gordon–Revel)
Lanny Ross in *College Rhythm* (1934)

STAY WITH ME (Ragovoy–Weiss)
Bette Midler in *The Rose* (1979)

STEAM HEAT (Ross–Adler)
Carol Haney in *The Pajama Game* (1957)

STEPPIN' OUT WITH MY BABY (Berlin)
Fred Astaire in *Easter Parade* (1948)

STEREOPHONIC SOUND (Porter)
Fred Astaire and Janis Paige in *Silk Stockings* (1957)

STORMY WEATHER (Arlen–Koehler)
Lena Horne in *Stormy Weather* (1943)
Connie Boswell in *Swing Parade Of 1946* (1946)

STOUT HEARTED MEN (Romberg–Hammerstein)
Lawrence Tibbett in *New Moon* (1930)
Nelson Eddy in *New Moon* (1940)

Helen Traubel in *Deep In My Heart* (1954)

STRANGER IN PARADISE (Wright–Forrest)
Vic Damone and Ann Blyth in *Kismet* (1955)

SUNDAY, MONDAY OR ALWAYS (Van Heusen–Burke)
Bing Crosby in *Dixie* (1943)

SUNNY SIDE UP (DeSylva–Brown–Henderson)
Charles Farrell and Janet Gaynor in *Sunny Side Up* (1929)

SUNRISE, SUNSET (Bock–Harnick)
Topol and Norma Crane in *Fiddler On The Roof* (1971)

SUPERSTAR (Webber–Rice)
Carl Anderson in *Jesus Christ Superstar* (1973)

THE SURREY WITH THE FRINGE ON THE TOP (Rodgers–Hammerstein)
Gordon MacRae and Shirley Jones in *Oklahoma* (1955)

SWANEE (Gershwin–Caesar)
Al Jolson in *Rhapsody In Blue* (1946)
Al Jolson for Larry Parks as Al Jolson in *The Jolson Story* (1946)
Judy Garland in *A Star Is Born* (1954)

SWEET AND LOVELY (Arnheim–Tobias–Lemare)
Harry James And His Orchestra with Helen Forrest, June Allyson and Gloria De Haven in *Two Girls And A Sailor* (1944)

SWEET DREAMS, SWEETHEART (Jerome–Koehler)
Kitty Carlisle in *Hollywood Canteen* (1944)

SWEET LEILANI (Owens)
Bing Crosby in *Waikiki Wedding* (1937)

SWEET ROSIE O'GRADY (Nugent)
Betty Grable and Robert Young in

Sweet Rosie O'Grady (1943)

SWINGIN' DOWN THE LANE (Jones–Kahn)
Vivian Blaine in *Greenwich Village* (1944)

SWINGING ON A STAR (Van Heusen–Burke)
Bing Crosby with the Robert Mitchell Boychoir in *Going My Way* (1944)

'S WONDERFUL (George and Ira Gershwin)
Gene Kelly and Georges Guetary in *An American In Paris* (1951)
Fred Astaire and Audrey Hepburn in *Funny Face* (1957)
Doris Day in *Starlift* (1951)

TAKE ME OUT TO THE BALL GAME (Tilzer–Norworth)
Dennis Morgan and Ann Sheridan in *Shine On Harvest Moon* (1944)
Gene Kelly, Frank Sinatra and Esther Williams in *Take Me Out To The Ball Game* (UK: *Everybody's Cheering*) (1948)

TAKING A CHANCE ON LOVE (Fetter–Latouche–Duke)
Ethel Waters in *Cabin In The Sky* (1943)
Lena Horne in *I Dood It* (1943)
June Haver and Gloria DeHaven in *I'll Get By* (1950)
Julie Wilson with Ray Anthony And His Orchestra in *This Could Be The Night* (1957)

TALK TO THE ANIMALS (Leslie Bricusse)
Rex Harrison and an assorted menagerie in *Doctor Dolittle* (1967)

TANGERINE (Schertzinger–Mercer)
Jimmy Dorsey And His Orchestra with Helen O'Connell and Bob Eberly in *The Fleet's In* (1942)

TEAMWORK (Van Heusen–Cahn)

Bing Crosby and Bob Hope in *Road To Hong Kong* (1962)

TEMPTATION (Brown–Freed)
Bing Crosby in *Going Hollywood* (1933)

TEN CENTS A DANCE (Rodgers–Hart)
Doris Day in *Love Me Or Leave Me* (1955)

THANK HEAVEN FOR LITTLE GIRLS (Lerner–Loewe)
Maurice Chevalier in *Gigi* (1958)

THANK YOUR LUCKY STARS (Loesser–Schwartz)
Dinah Shore in *Thank Your Lucky Stars* (1943)

THANKS FOR THE MEMORY (Rainger–Robin)
Bob Hope and Shirley Ross in *The Big Broadcast Of 1938* (1937)

THAT OLD BLACK MAGIC (Arlen–Mercer)
Johnnie Johnston in *Star Spangled Rhythm* (1942)

Bing Crosby in *Here Come The Waves* (1944)

Frank Sinatra in *Meet Danny Wilson* (1952)

Marilyn Monroe in *Bus Stop* (1956)

THAT OLD FEELING (Fain–Brown)

Virginia Verrill in *Vogues Of 1938* (1937)

Jane Froman for Susan Hayward as Jane Froman in *With A Song In My Heart* (1952)

THAT'S ENTERTAINMENT (Schwartz–Deitz)

Fred Astaire, Nanette Fabray, India Adams, Jack Buchanan and Oscar Levant in *The Band Wagon* (1953)

The original sequence included in the 1974 MGM compilation *That's Entertainment* and sung by Fred Astaire and Gene Kelly (the hosts) in *That's Entertainment Part 2* (1976)

THAT'S FOR ME (Rodgers–Hammerstein)

Vivian Blaine in *State Fair* (1945)

Pat Boone in *State Fair* (1962)

THEME FROM "NEW YORK, NEW YORK" (Kander–Ebb)

Liza Minnelli in *New York, New York* (1977)

THERE GOES THAT SONG AGAIN (Styne–Cahn)

Harry Babbitt and Kay Kyser And His Orchestra in *Carolina Blues* (1944)

Dick Haymes in *Cruisin' Down The River* (1953)

THERE WILL NEVER BE ANOTHER YOU (Warren–Gordon)

Joan Merrill in *Iceland* (1942)

Dennis Day in *I'll Get By* (1950)

THERE'LL BE SOME CHANGES MADE (Overstreet–Higgins)

Ann Reinking in the 1979 movie *All That Jazz*

THERE'S A LULL IN MY LIFE (Revel–Gordon)

Alice Faye in *Wake Up And Live* (1937)

THERE'S A RAINBOW ROUND MY SHOULDER (Rose–Dryer–Jolson)

Al Jolson in *The Singing Fool* (1928)

Al Jolson for Larry Parks as Al Jolson in *The Jolson Story* (1946)

THERE'S A SMALL HOTEL (Rodgers–Hart)

Betty Garrett in *Words And Music* (1949)

Frank Sinatra in *Pal Joey* (1957)

THERE'S NO BUSINESS LIKE SHOW BUSINESS (Berlin)

Betty Hutton, Howard Keel, Keenan Wynn and Louis Calhern in *Annie Get Your Gun* (1950)

Ethel Merman, Dan Dailey, Marilyn Monroe, Donald O'Connor, Mitzi Gaynor and Johnnie Ray in *There's No Business Like Show Business* (1954)

THEY ALL LAUGHED (George and Ira Gershwin)

Ginger Rogers in *Shall We Dance* (1937)

THEY CAN'T TAKE THAT AWAY FROM ME (George and Ira Gershwin)

Fred Astaire in *Shall We Dance* (1937)

Fred Astaire in *The Barkleys Of Broadway* (1949)

THEY'RE EITHER TOO YOUNG OR TOO OLD (Loesser–Schwartz)

Bette Davis in *Thank Your Lucky Stars* (1943)

Jane Froman for Susan Hayward as Jane Froman in *With A Song In My Heart* (1952)

THEY'RE WEARING THEM HIGHER IN HAWAII (Mohr–

Goodwin)
George Murphy in *Show Business* (1944)

THINGS ARE LOOKING UP (George and Ira Gershwin)
Fred Astaire in *A Damsel In Distress* (1937)

THIS CAN'T BE LOVE (Rodgers–Hart)
Rosemary Lane in *The Boys From Syracuse* (1940)

THIS HEART OF MINE (Warren–Freed)
Fred Astaire in *Ziegfeld Follies* (1946)

THOROUGHLY MODERN MILLIE (Van Heusen–Cahn)
Julie Andrews in *Thoroughly Modern Millie* (1967)

THOU SWELL (Rodgers–Hart)
June Allyson in *Words And Music* (1948)

THREE LITTLE WORDS (Kalmar–Ruby)
Bing Crosby in *Check And Double Check* (1930)
Fred Astaire in *Three Little Words* (1950)

THREE O'CLOCK IN THE MORNING (Robledo–Terris)
Judy Garland in *Presenting Lily Mars* (1943)
Jeanne Crain in *Margie* (1946)

THRILLER (Temperton)
Michael Jackson (and dialogue by Vincent Price) in the musical short *Thriller* (1983)

TICKET TO RIDE (Lennon–McCartney)
The Beatles in *Help!* (1965)

TIGER RAG (LaRocca)
The Mills Brothers in *The Big Broadcast* (1932)

TILL THERE WAS YOU (Willson)
Robert Preston and Shirley Jones in *The Music Man* (1962)

TIME AFTER TIME (Styne–Cahn)
Frank Sinatra in *It Happened In Brooklyn* (1947)

THE TIME WARP (O'Brien)
Tim Curry in *The Rocky Horror Picture Show* (1975)

TIP-TOE THRU THE TULIPS WITH ME (Burke–Dubin)
Nick Lucas in *Gold Diggers Of Broadway* (1929)

TO ME (Wrubel–George)
Janet Blair, Tommy Dorsey And His Orchestra in *The Fabulous Dorseys* (1947)

TOMORROW (Strouse–Charnin)
Aileen Quinn in *Annie* (1981)

TONIGHT (Bernstein–Sondheim)
Jim Bryant for Richard Beymer and Marni Nixon for Natalie Wood in *West Side Story* (1961)

TOO MARVELOUS FOR WORDS (Whiting–Mercer)
Ruby Keeler, Lee Dixon, Winifred Shaw and Ross Alexander in *Ready, Willing And Able* (1937)
Doris Day in *Young Man With A Horn* (1950)

TOO ROMANTIC (Monaco–Burke)
Bing Crosby and Dorothy Lamour in *Road To Singapore* (1940)

TOO-RA-LOO-RA-LOO-RAL (THAT'S AN IRISH LULLABY) (Shannon)
Bing Crosby in *Going My Way* (1944)

TOOT, TOOT, TOOTSIE, GOODBYE (Russo–Erdman)
Al Jolson in *The Jazz Singer* (1927)
Al Jolson in *Rose Of Washington Square* (1939)
Doris Day in *I'll See You In My Dreams* (1951)

TOP HAT, WHITE TIE AND TAILS (Berlin)
Fred Astaire in *Top Hat* (1935)

THE TROLLEY SONG (Martin–Blane)

Bing Crosby croons "True Love" to Grace Kelly in *High Society* (1956).

Judy Garland and a chorus of streetcar passengers in *Meet Me In St. Louis* (1944)

TRUE LOVE (Porter)
Bing Crosby and Grace Kelly in *High Society* (1956)

TWO DREAMS MET (Warren–Gordon)
Don Ameche to Betty Grable in *Down Argentine Way* (1940)

TWO SLEEPY PEOPLE (Loesser–Carmichael)
Bob Hope and Shirley Ross in *Thanks For The Memory* (1938)

THE VARSITY DRAG (DeSylva–Brown–Henderson)
Dorothy McNulty (Penny Singleton) in *Good News* (1930)
June Allyson and Peter Lawford in *Good News* (1947)

WAIT TILL THE SUN SHINES, NELLIE (Tilzer–Sterling)
Bing Crosby and Mary Martin in *Birth Of The Blues* (1941)

THE WAITER AND THE PORTER AND THE UPSTAIRS MAID (Mercer)
Bing Crosby, Mary Martin and Jack Teagarden in *Birth Of The Blues* (1941)

WAKE UP AND LIVE (Revel–Gordon)
Alice Faye in *Wake Up And Live* (1937)

WANDRIN' STAR (Lerner–Loewe)
Lee Marvin in *Paint Your Wagon* (1969)

THE WAY HE MAKES ME FEEL (Legrand–A. and M. Bergman)
Barbra Streisand in *Yentl* (1983)

THE WAY YOU LOOK TONIGHT (Kern–Fields)
Fred Astaire to Ginger Rogers in *Swing Time* (1936)

WE'RE IN THE MONEY (THE GOLD DIGGERS' SONG) (Warren–Dubin)
Ginger Rogers in *Gold Diggers Of 1933* (1933)
Dennis Morgan and Chorus in *Painting The Clouds With Sunshine* (1951)

WE'RE OFF TO SEE THE WIZARD (Arlen–Harburg)
Judy Garland, Ray Bolger, Jack Haley and Bert Lahr in *The Wizard Of Oz* (1939)

THE WEDDING OF THE PAINTED DOLL (Brown–Freed)
James Burrows in *Broadway Melody* (1929)

WELL DID YOU EVAH (Porter)
Bing Crosby and Frank Sinatra in *High Society* (1956)

WHAT IS THIS THING CALLED LOVE? (Porter)
Ginny Simms in *Night And Day* (1946)
Gordon MacRae and Lucille Norman in *Starlift* (1951)

WHATEVER LOLA WANTS (Ross–Adler)
Gwen Verdon in *Damn Yankees* (UK: *What Lola Wants*) (1958)

WHEN I GROW TOO OLD TO DREAM (Romberg–Hammerstein)
Ramon Novarro and Evelyn Laye in *The Night Is Young* (1935)
Jose Ferrer to Doe Avedon in *Deep In My Heart* (1954)

WHEN IRISH EYES ARE SMILING (Olcott–Ball–Graff)
Betty Grable in *Coney Island* (1943)
Dick Haymes to June Haver in *Irish Eyes Are Smiling* (1944)
Dennis Morgan in *My Wild Irish Rose* (1947)

WHEN THE MIDNIGHT CHOO-CHOO LEAVES FOR ALABAM (Berlin)
Judy Garland and Fred Astaire in *Easter Parade* (1948)
Ethel Merman and Dan Dailey in *There's No Business Like Show Business* (1954)

WHEN THE MOON COMES OVER THE MOUNTAIN (Woods–Johnson–Smith)
Kate Smith in *The Big Broadcast* (1932)

WHEN THE RED, RED ROBIN COMES BOB, BOB, BOBBIN' ALONG (Woods)
Susan Hayward as Lillian Roth in *I'll Cry Tomorrow* (1955)

WHEN YOU WISH UPON A STAR (Harline–Washington)
Cliff Edwards for the cartoon character, Jiminy Cricket, in *Pinocchio* (1940)

WHEN YOU WORE A TULIP AND I WORE A BIG RED ROSE (Wenrich–Mahoney)
Allan Jones in *Larceny With Music* (1943)
Ann Blyth in *The Merry Monahans* (1944)

WHERE OR WHEN (Rodgers–Hart)

Cliff Edwards provided the voice for Jiminy Cricket's appealing "When You Wish Upon A Star" in the animated musical *Pinocchio*.

Judy Garland in *Babes In Arms* (1937)

Lena Horne in *Words And Music* (1948)

WHERE THE BLUE OF THE NIGHT MEETS THE GOLD OF THE DAY (Ahlert–Turk–Crosby)
Bing Crosby in *The Big Broadcast* (1932)

WHERE YOU ARE (Warren–Gordon)
Alice Faye in *The Great American Broadcast* (1941)

WHISTLE WHILE YOU WORK (Churchill–Morey)
Adriana Caselotti for the cartoon character Snow White in *Snow White And The Seven Dwarfs* (1937)

WHITE CHRISTMAS (Berlin)
Bing Crosby with Martha Mears for Marjorie Reynolds in *Holiday Inn* (1942)
Bing Crosby in *Blue Skies* (1946)
Bing Crosby, Danny Kaye, Rose-

mary Clooney and Vera-Ellen in *White Christmas* (1954)

WHO (Kern–Hammerstein–Harbach)
Marilyn Miller in *Sunny* (1930)
Anna Neagle in *Sunny* (1941)
Judy Garland in *Till The Clouds Roll By* (1946)
Ray Bolger in *Look For The Silver Lining* (1949)

WHO WANTS TO BE A MILLIONAIRE? (Porter)
Frank Sinatra and Celeste Holm in *High Society* (1956)

WHO'S SORRY NOW (Snyder–Kalmar–Ruby)
Gloria De Haven in *Three Little Words* (1950)

WHY DO I DREAM THOSE DREAMS (Warren–Dubin)
Dick Powell in *Wonder Bar* (1934)

WITH A SONG IN MY HEART (Rodgers–Hart)
Bernice Clare and Alexander Gray in *Spring Is Here* (1930)
Perry Como in *Words And Music* (1948)
Dennis Morgan in *Painting The Clouds With Sunshine* (1951)
Jane Froman for Susan Hayward as Jane Froman in *With A Song In My Heart* (1952)

WITH PLENTY OF MONEY AND YOU (Warren–Dubin)
Dick Powell (singing before the main titles) in *Gold Diggers Of 1937* (1937)
Doris Day in *My Dream Is Yours* (1949)

A WOMAN IN LOVE (Loesser)
Marlon Brando to Jean Simmons in *Guys And Dolls* (1955)

WONDERFUL, WONDERFUL DAY (DePaul–Mercer)
Jane Powell in *Seven Brides For Seven Brothers* (1954)

WOODEN HEART (Kaempfert–Wise–Weisman)

Elvis Presley to Juliet Prowse in *GI Blues* (1960)

THE WORDS ARE IN MY HEART (Warren–Dubin)
Dick Powell to Gloria Stuart in *Gold Diggers Of 1935* (1935)

WOULD YOU (Brown–Freed)
Jeanette MacDonald to Clark Gable in *San Francisco* (1936)

WUNDERBAR (Porter)
Kathryn Grayson and Howard Keel in *Kiss Me Kate* (1953)

YANKEE DOODLE BOY (Cohan)
James Cagney as George M. Cohan in *Yankee Doodle Dandy* (1942)
James Cagney as George M. Cohan in *Seven Little Foys* (1955)

YES SIR, THAT'S MY BABY (Donaldson–Kahn)
Danny Thomas and Doris Day in *I'll See You In My Dreams* (1951)
Eddie Cantor for Keefe Brasselle as Eddie Cantor in *The Eddie Cantor Story* (1953)

YOU ARE MY LUCKY STAR (Brown–Freed)
Frances Langford in *Broadway Melody Of 1936* (1935)
Betty Janes in *Babes In Arms* (1939)
Phil Regan in *Three Little Words* (1950)
Gene Kelly and Debbie Reynolds in *Singin' In The Rain* (1952)
Twiggy in *The Boy Friend* (1971)
Liza Minnelli in *New York, New York* (1976)

YOU BROUGHT A NEW KIND OF LOVE TO ME (Fain–Norman–Kahal)
Maurice Chevalier to Claudette Colbert in *The Big Pond* (1930)
Liza Minnelli in *New York, New York* (1976)

YOU CAN'T GET A MAN WITH A GUN (Berlin)

Susan Hayward won a Picturegoer Gold Medal for her performance as Jane Froman in *With A Song In My Heart* (1952).

Betty Hutton in *Annie Get Your Gun* (1950)

YOU DO SOMETHING TO ME (Porter)
Ginny Simms in *Night And Day* (1946)
Doris Day in *Starlift* (1951)
Mario Lanza in *Because You're Mine* (1952)
Gogi Grant for Ann Blyth as Helen Morgan in *The Helen*

Morgan Story (UK: *Both Ends Of The Candle*) (1957)

Louis Jourdan in *Can-Can* (1961)

YOU DON'T HAVE TO KNOW THE LANGUAGE (Van Heusen–Burke)

Bing Crosby and The Andrews Sisters in *Road To Rio* (1947)

YOU MADE ME LOVE YOU (Monaco–McCarthy)

Al Jolson for Larry Parks in *The Jolson Story* (1946)

Doris Day in *Love Me Or Leave Me* (1946)

Adapted as "Dear Mr Gable" for Judy Garland in *Broadway Melody Of 1938* (1937)

YOU MUST HAVE BEEN A BEAUTIFUL BABY (Warren–Mercer)

Dick Powell to Olivia De Havilland in *Hard To Get* (1938)

Doris Day in *My Dream Is Yours* (1949)

YOU NEVER LOOKED SO BEAUTIFUL BEFORE (Donaldson)

Judy Garland in *Ziegfeld Girl* (1941)

YOU OUGHTA BE IN PICTURES (Suesse–Heyman)

Doris Day in *Starlift* (1951)

YOU STEPPED OUT OF A DREAM (Brown–Kahn)

Tony Martin in *Ziegfeld Girl* (1941)

YOU WERE MEANT FOR ME (Brown–Freed)

Charles King in *Broadway Melody* (1929)

Anita Page in *Hollywood Revue* (1929)

Winnie Lightner in *Show Of Shows* (1929)

Dan Dailey in *You Were Meant For Me* (1948)

Gene Kelly in *Singin' In The Rain* (1952)

YOU WERE NEVER LOVELIER (Kern–Mercer)

Fred Astaire to Rita Hayworth in *You Were Never Lovelier* (1942)

YOU'D BE SO HARD TO REPLACE (Warren–Gershwin)

Fred Astaire to Ginger Rogers in *The Barkleys Of Broadway* (1950)

YOU'D BE SO NICE TO COME HOME TO (Porter)

Don Ameche and Janet Blair in *Something To Shout About* (1943)

YOU'LL NEVER KNOW (Warren–Gordon)

Alice Faye in *Hello, Frisco, Hello* (1943)

Alice Faye in *Four Jills And A Jeep* (1944)

YOU'LL NEVER WALK ALONE (Rodgers–Hammerstein)

Claramae Turner in *Carousel* (1956)

YOU'RE GETTING TO BE A HABIT WITH ME (Warren–Dubin)

Bebe Daniels in *42nd Street* (1933)

Doris Day in *Lullaby Of Broadway* (1951)

YOU'RE JUST IN LOVE (Berlin)

Ethel Merman and Donald O'Connor in *Call Me Madam* (1953)

YOU'RE MY EVERYTHING (Warren–Young–Dixon)

Dan Dailey in *You're My Everything* (1949)

Played by Carmen Cavallaro for Tyrone Power as Eddy Duchin in *The Eddy Duchin Story* (1956)

YOU'RE SENSATIONAL (Porter)

Frank Sinatra in *High Society* (1956)

YOU'RE THE ONE THAT I WANT (Farrar)

Olivia Newton-John and John Travolta in *Grease* (1978)

YOU'RE THE TOP (Porter)

Ethel Merman and Bing Crosby in *Anything Goes* (1936)

Bing Crosby and Mitzi Gaynor in

Alice Faye sang "You'll Never Know" in the period musical, *Hello, Frisco, Hello* (1943).

Anything Goes (1956)
Ginny Simms and Cary Grant in *Night And Day* (1946)
YOUNG AND HEALTHY (Warren–Dubin)
Dick Powell to Toby Wing in *42nd Street* (1933)
YOUNG AT HEART (Richards–Leigh)
Frank Sinatra in *Young At Heart* (1955)

ZING! WENT THE STRINGS OF MY HEART (Hanley)
Judy Garland in *Listen, Darling* (1938)
Gene Nelson in *Lullaby Of Broadway* (1951)
ZING, ZING, ZING A LITTLE ZONG (Warren–Robin)
Bing Crosby and Jane Wyman in *Just For You* (1952)

INDEX OF SONG TITLES

INDEX OF ARTISTS

INDEX OF MOVIES AND TELEVISION PROGRAMMES

Thunder Road 47, 91
Thunderball 50
Till The Clouds Roll By 35, 106, 111,
 116, 117, 118, 122, 136
Till The End Of Time 17, 21
The Time, The Place And The Girl
 106
Times Square Lady 86
Tin Pan Alley 7, 109, 120, 126
Titanic 85
To Be Or Not To Be 89
To Each His Own 59
To Have And Have Not 74, 80, 95
To Sir, With Love 48
Toast Of New Orleans 100
The Toast Of New York 80
Together? 54
Tommy 97, 123
Tonight And Every Night 93
Tony Rome 48
Too Many Girls 81
Tootsie 55, 84
Top Hat 103, 115, 121, 123, 133
Topper 86
A Touch Of Class 72
Towering Inferno 90
Town Without Pity 48
The Trail Of The Lonesome Pine 84,
 90
The Travels Of Jamie McPheeters 69
Tribute To A Badman 81
Trouble Man 48
True Confessions 30
True Grit 48
True To The Army 110, 117
Tumbling Tumbleweeds 90
Twenty Million Sweethearts 21, 112
Two Girls And A Sailor 82, 97, 130
Two Of A Kind 57
2001: A Space Odyssey 15
Two Weeks In Another Town 79
Two Weeks With Love 97

Unchained 2, 48
Unfaithfully Yours 48
Unholy Partners 72
The Uninvited 63
Up In Smoke 48

Urban Cowboy 53, 55, 84

The Vagabond King 123
Valentino 70
Valley Of The Dolls 48, 95
Vertigo 60
The Very Thought Of You 21
Victor, Victoria 115
The Victors 29
Victory At Sea 67
Virginia City 87
Viva Las Vegas 108
Vogues of 1938 132
Voices 94
Voyage Of The Damned 29

Wagon Master 20
Wagon Train 66
Waikiki Wedding 101, 130
Wake Up And Dream 107
Wake Up And Live 94, 121, 132, 135
Walk On The Wild Side 48
The Wanderers 27
The War Wagon 48
Watership Down 53
Way Out West 75, 90
The Way We Were 48
Wedding Bells 109
Weekend At The Waldorf 74
Welcome Back, Kotter 69
Welcome To LA 78
We're Not Dressing 118
West Side Story 95, 119, 133
Westward Ho, The Wagons! 58
What Lola Wants 135
What Price Glory 38
What's New Pussycat 48
What's Up Doc 75
Whatever Happened To Baby Jane 82
When Irish Eyes Are Smiling 116
When The Boys Meet The Girls 102
Where Love Has Gone 48
Where The Boys Are 48
Where's Charley 122
White Christmas 101, 103, 136
Who'll Stop The Rain 33
Who's Minding The Store? 32
Whoopee 118, 120

Wild In The Country 48
Wild Is The Wind 49
Willy Wonka And The Chocolate
 Factory 97
A Window To The Sky 56
With A Song In My Heart 35, 94,
 101, 102, 105, 107, 108, 112, 113,
 132, 136
Witness For The Prosecution 81
Wives And Lovers 60
The Wiz 105
The Wizard Of Oz 3, 104, 114, 123,
 135
A Woman Commands 86
A Woman's Secret 86
Women In Love 36
Wonder Bar 86, 104, 136
Wonder Man 86
Words And Music 101, 111, 115, 116,
 119, 132, 133, 136
The World According To Garp 31
Written On The Wind 49
Wyatt Earp 66

A Yank In The RAF 37
Yankee Doodle Dandy 108, 115, 123,
 137
Yanks 30
The Yellow Rolls-Royce 54
Yellow Submarine 41
Yentl 135
You Came Along 32, 91
You Light Up My Life 94
You Only Live Twice 50
You Were Meant For Me 112, 114,
 138
You Were Never Lovelier 104, 138
You're A Big Boy Now 53
You're My Everything 103, 138
The Young And The Restless 67
Young At Heart 116, 122, 139
Young Frankenstein 87
Young Man With A Horn 93, 111,133
Young Widow 37

Ziegfeld Follies 117, 133
Ziegfeld Girl 120, 138
Zorro 69